# FROM THE BORDER
# TO THE BOARDROOM

# FROM THE BORDER TO THE BOARDROOM

*A Journey from Poverty to Passionate Purpose*

GRISELDA CASTRO ABOUSLEMAN

**PALMETTO**
PUBLISHING
Charleston, SC
www.PalmettoPublishing.com

Copyright © 2024 by Griselda Castro Abousleman

All rights reserved
No portion of this book may be reproduced, stored in a retrieval system, or transmitted in any form by any means–electronic, mechanical, photocopy, recording, or other– except for brief quotations in printed reviews, without prior permission of the author.

Hardback ISBN: 979-8-8229-6187-6
Paperback ISBN: 979-8-8229-6182-1
eBook ISBN: 979-8-8229-6183-8
AudioBook ISBN: 979-8-8229-6184-5

# DEDICATION

To my mom, Sandra, who has taught my siblings and me so much about life, resilience, family unity, and how to truly love one another, like she loved my father. It is also written in his memory, as he is always with me in heart, mind, and soul. Through this book, I'm on a mission to ensure Mom knows exactly what their caring, loving nature did for us. As they loved and cared for one another, we learned about life.

To my husband, Greg, as I wrote this with intent to inform the world that there are many strong men, like my Greg, that will support, encourage, challenge, and propel their partner into achieving whatever they set their mind to. This growth mindset is what he displays in his personal life. I see it in our three children and in his eyes. As I stare into those determined eyes, I know that there is hope that many men and women will support each other to achieve great things in life.

And finally, to my dear children.

To Briana, whose energetic enthusiasm about fitness, nutrition, and health keeps all of us shining.

To Gabriela, who inspires me to keep expanding my knowledge in STEM and thrives in being a lively competitor in all she does.

To Gregory, whose positivity and genuine optimism are constant reminders that everything in life is possible when you dedicate your heart and mind to it.

# TABLE OF CONTENTS

Introduction . . . . . . . . . . . . . . . . . . . . . . . . . . . . . . . 1

### Part One: A Brave Pioneer's Story
1: Life Is What You Make of It. . . . . . . . . . . . . . . . . . . 5
2: Sacrifice and Perseverance Pay Off in Big Ways . . . . . . 13
3: Face Your Fears with Courage and Hope . . . . . . . . . . . 21
4: In Pursuit of the American Dream . . . . . . . . . . . . . . . 29

### Part Two: From the Rio Grande Valley to the Farm
5: A Strong Community Moves Forward . . . . . . . . . . . . . 39
6: Engage Others on Your Trail. . . . . . . . . . . . . . . . . . . 45
7: Persist with Relentless Passion . . . . . . . . . . . . . . . . . 55
8: Helpfulness Matters . . . . . . . . . . . . . . . . . . . . . . . . 63
9: Appreciate Your Advocates, Especially the Tough Ones 73

### Part Three: Life after the Farm
10: Life Is Not Fair, Make the Best of It. . . . . . . . . . . . . 93
11: When Life Happens, Embrace Optimism. . . . . . . . . . 103
12: It's a Journey, not a Destination. . . . . . . . . . . . . . . . 113
13: Life in the Boardroom. . . . . . . . . . . . . . . . . . . . . . 121
14: Ignite Your Passion! . . . . . . . . . . . . . . . . . . . . . . . 131

Appendix: Mom's Recipes! . . . . . . . . . . . . . . . . . . . . . 135
Acknowledgements . . . . . . . . . . . . . . . . . . . . . . . . . . 147
About the Author . . . . . . . . . . . . . . . . . . . . . . . . . . 149

# INTRODUCTION

All of us get punched in the gut or slapped on the face with challenging events and adversity at some point in life, and many times when it's least expected. You've probably heard or read the usual phrases of encouragement: when the going gets tough, the tough get going; move on with confidence; and what doesn't kill you makes you stronger. Well, the truth is we must OWN our life's choices and take swift action for this rejuvenating strength to come alive!

This book is about two women's struggles and accomplishments through the meandering river of life. I will share with you my life's story, one that ebbs and flows through the inevitable adversities we all experience, some more than others. I am no different than you, and I can attest that whatever the circumstances you face, you can also overcome them with perseverance, hope, drive, and courage.

When I say meandering river, I truly mean that, as this story starts by the ever-flowing waters of a river that makes numerous headlines these days—the Rio Grande River in the southernmost tip of Texas. It begins in a Mexican border city called Matamoros, Tamaulipas, and winds its way to the humble, friendly, and, at times, melancholic city of Brownsville, Texas. I say that because of the many hardships that are endured by its residents due to being a growing city on the border of the Texas—Mexico Rio Grande Valley.

Our experiences will make you laugh, cry, reflect, and hopefully take action. So if you, like me, have ever had financial struggles, challenges at school, or a bad review at work, if you went through a divorce, had trouble bearing children, or gave life to a special someone who was diagnosed with "failure to thrive" or some other unique diagnosis, or if you are simply struggling with the rat race trying to balance family and career life, this book is for you.

I know in my heart that you will relate to some of it, and most importantly that you'll enjoy the reality that comes to life as you flip through these pages…and ultimately, be INSPIRED to take action for your best self. So let's start this journey together!

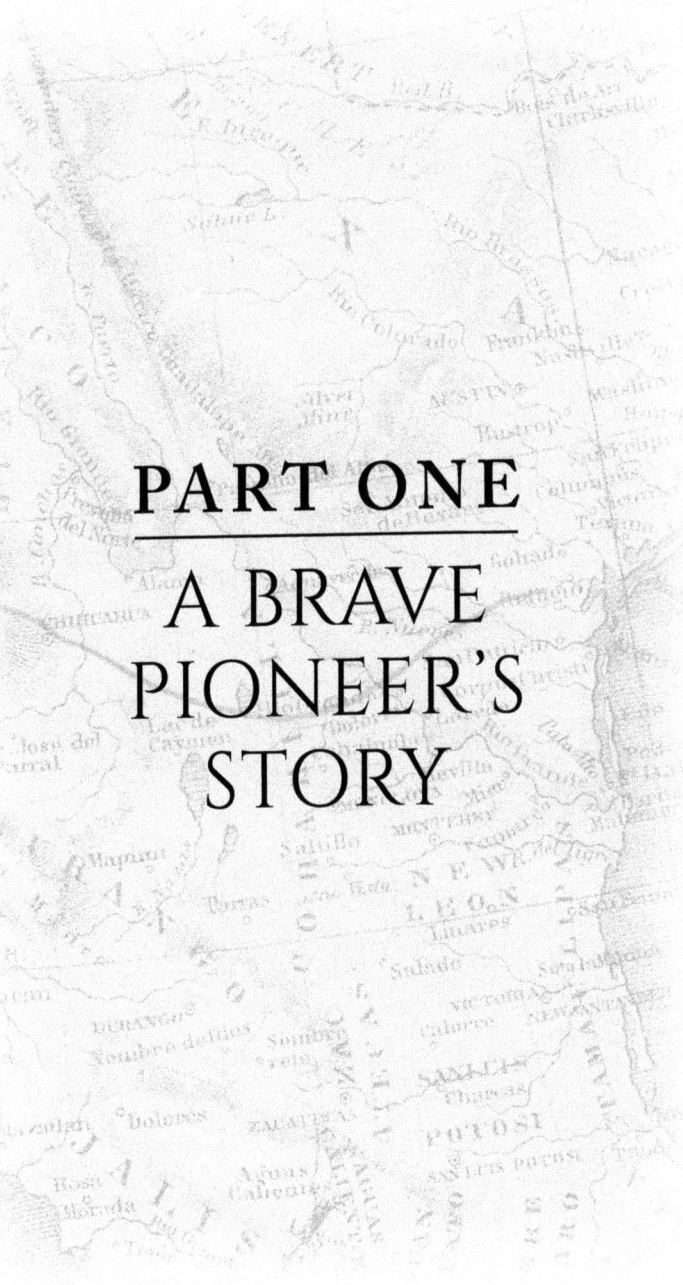

# PART ONE
# A BRAVE PIONEER'S STORY

# 1
# LIFE IS WHAT YOU MAKE OF IT

Beatriz Cortéz Montejano was a determined and strong woman who managed to make it through the early beginnings of married life and her childbearing years by learning from her friends and neighbors. She would help her friends and neighbors with giving birth to their children, and in essence, she became a self-taught midwife. She knew she lived in extreme poverty and feared that if she ever had her own children, she would not have the means to visit a hospital or clinic to give birth. She would have to deliver her children herself, and therefore, she needed to be trained. She helped others with a loving heart, knowing that someday she, too, would need that help and support from others. Well, one bright, sunny afternoon, that day finally came! Beatriz gave birth to a healthy and darling baby boy. I state it this way because that is exactly what happened. She felt contractions, knew how to time them to determine when she'd be ready to push her baby out, and had prepared all the sheets, towels, scissors, and warm water to help herself through the process. There was nobody else there; no one was available to help her give life to this vibrant child inside of her. That did not matter. She went through the process on the hard floor of the one-room home that she rented from her neighbor, and gave birth to her first child. These were the early years of my grandmother's life just south of the US-Mexico border in Matamoros, Tamaulipas, Mexico.

One cold winter night, Beatriz was cuddled up in a corner of her one-room home. She was using every inch of her body to warm her young child battling the measles virus at the tender age of eighteen months. The one-room wooden home was plagued with numerous holes in the wall that allowed every whisper of cold air and humidity to creep in to chill the bones throughout her body and her child's tiny existence. Back in the 1940s, my grandmother Beatriz did not have access to vaccines or medications that could help heal her child. The measles virus was so widespread in the 1940s and '50s with no sign of vaccines to stop the spread. This pre vaccine era was a major challenge for many families living in poverty. Life in Mexico was a daily and constant challenge for her, as it was for many women in those days. She worked from dawn to dusk just to be able to feed herself, her husband, and her child, and to be able to pay the rent in this tiny place she called home.

Her husband, my grandfather, was an adventurous man. He was a talented musician who loved to sing and play string instruments at various bars and restaurants that would pay him a decent amount for entertainment. He was a master at the violin and the guitar, and had a great singing voice. I guess these talents are part of what my grandmother saw in him when she fell in love with my grandfather, Benjamin. Little did she know that these talents would also be what kept him away from his family and home for days on end…sometimes weeks. Grandpa loved his drinking, and his music, and who knows what else, but let's just say that he was not always around to protect my grandmother and her virus-stricken son. Don't take me wrong, male readers, there will be exemplary men that come up later in this book; I just can't claim that my maternal grandfather was one of them, not initially at least.

As the cold air and freezing nights rolled on, Grandma Beatriz did the best she could to protect her son while she still worked at her boss, Doña Reyes's, house. She could not pay rent during these challenging moments, so she wrapped up her son, and took him with her to Doña Reyes's house to clean, wash clothes, iron, and do anything else that her boss and her family needed in exchange for my grandmother's use of their humble one-room abode. During one of those painfully cold days, she cuddled him to protect him from the cold wind that crept into her home. Morning sunrise broke through, and her child's condition only worsened. She tried feeding him, holding him, and keeping him warm. She prayed for the sun to shine brighter and warm up her place. She prayed for a miraculous recovery and that those nasty red blotches of rash that plagued his tender skin would just disappear. She cried, she prayed, she loved, and then she unwrapped her young child from his protective swaddle blanket, only to find that he was freezing cold too, literally. Her firstborn son only lived for eighteen months before the measles outbreak took his tiny body into heaven.

Life as she knew it continued for young Beatriz, and due to her lack of birth control access or education to protect herself, over a year later, she was blessed with another young boy. She was ready for this one, she felt. She had saved up some money to be able to protect her son and rest with him if he needed to be cared for during unhealthy times. Another bright idea she had come up with was to patch up the holes all around the wooden home. Grandmother Beatriz was resourceful—with whatever challenges she faced, she found solutions, and strength. She had taken some time during her evenings to gather outdated calendars and good old duct tape to cover the holes. She even felt the warmth during those cold winter nights! Of course, the heat of summer also plagued their tiny home, but for those days, she simply stepped outside under some shade for fresh air.

Unfortunately, her second son was also taken at the very tender age of fourteen months by the same demonic virus, the measles. I will not go into detail as to how this second parting took place, but let's just say that it was just as painful and even more devastating than the first one. She had prepared, she was ready, and her efforts to protect him ultimately did not prove successful. She feared the nights that my grandfather would come home, after drinking into the late hours, and she would have to relay such news to him. They were not ready for the hardship of burying their own sons and giving them a proper faithful parting into their next life. However, without the help of her own husband, she did exactly that and said goodbye to the love of her life, once again.

As the years passed, Grandmother Beatriz kept praying, working, and helping others. She knew one day she'd be blessed with a surviving, strong child, and she'd have someone to cuddle and protect for many years to come. On June 21, 1946, that dream came true. She gave birth, on her own again (she was getting good at this process), to a beautiful baby girl named Maria Isaura. She was determined to do everything in her power to protect her daughter, but was also realistic, knowing that any one of the many viruses or diseases out there could easily strip her of her offspring in seconds. It had happened before, and therefore she knew that her faith and her prayers were all she had to get through the days of raising beautiful young Isaura.

Isaura grew up to be a tenacious and loving helper, just like her mom. As soon as she was able to, she helped keep their tiny home clean, she would help her mom with the housecleaning and laundry at Doña Reyes's house, and she learned how to do these things herself. Her happiness stemmed from just helping her mom, and my grandmother's pride and joy came from watching Isaura blossom. They both felt immense dedication to one another, and their bond grew stronger every day. Guess what else Isaura was able to learn from her mom? You guessed it, how to deliver a child on a hard wooden floor, just the basics, enough so that she would not be totally surprised by the process. Now, this is not something my grandmother wanted her to be a part of, but it was something she needed to prepare her for in case they were left alone when she gave birth to any future children. Luckily for Isaura, and my grandmother, although this day did come when her daughter was only four years old, this time, Grandmother Beatriz did have help from a friend to ensure that Isaura was safe and outside of the house while she gave birth to Carmelita, her fourth child.

Now they were three, living mostly alone. Grandfather Benjamin came in and out as he pleased, and Grandmother Beatriz ensured the girls were safe. Grandma's life was filled with joy even as she worked ten to twelve hours a day in her landlord's home, while she cared for her own two girls. She prepared their breakfast, they ate together, then she went off to serve their landlord for the rest of the day, leaving only a few hours at night to feed her girls again, and repeat the routine. She was grateful to Doña Reyes for allowing her to take her daughters with her while she labored. At times they would help, but mostly they would play outside in the dirt yard when Carmelita was able to walk on her own. Isaura did her best to take care of her little sister. She had not experienced the hardships that her mom had suffered in previous years. During one fine morning as they prepared for the day, Grandmother Beatriz saw a slight rash on Carmelita's face. With tears in her eyes, she said a prayer, and then protected both girls, while keeping them distant, as she knew what was ahead of her. There was no way to prepare a young child like Isaura for what was to come. It was just life, and her daughter Isaura would also have to face the challenges that life brought upon them. On a dark summer night, the measles virus also took Carmelita's life. This parting was especially hard for Grandma Beatriz as she had to share the pain with her daughter Isaura. The mother-daughter bond only grew stronger as they both said farewell to a darling, innocent angel.

## LIFE IS WHAT YOU MAKE OF IT—REFLECTIONS

Let's reflect on Grandmother Beatriz's life and what she made of it. She had full **awareness** of her situation. She lived in poverty, with a musician husband that loved his women and drinking, and was rarely ever home to protect her. She was also **self-aware** that she had to overcome this life and make the best of it, for her own good and the good of her children. Life would be hard, but that only meant she had to stay strong.

She also knew that she had to **acquire skills** to make it in life. Her first survival skills were not only working in house cleaning and laundry, but eventually sewing, which she learned from the women whose homes she cleaned. She was **increasing her value** with every skill she learned, without much training, all through attentive observation. Even her desire to learn how to give birth to her own children, as painful as that was, showed that she was aware of the physical and emotional pain, and she knew the steps she had to follow to ensure her children's livelihood. The emotional pain of "sending them off to heaven" was even more painful than the physical suffering of giving birth, but that was another skill she learned—how to physically, and emotionally, bury her children with blessings for preparation into another life, a more perfect one.

Grandmother Beatriz was also **resourceful**. She used whatever she could find to fill the voids around her home and try to create less coldness in her humble home. She found ways to overcome challenges in everything she did in life, and that resourcefulness kept her alive.

Finally, she had extreme **perseverance** with a **balanced acceptance**. She persevered through all the challenges that came her way. She figured it out. There was no whining or giving up or moping that happened. It would be to no avail. Who would even listen? She persevered through her numerous challenges, no matter how emotionally painful they were, and this only strengthened her heart and mind. The balanced acceptance was also clear. Although devastated, she knew that there was no vaccine to help her cure her sick children when the measles virus struck home. She cared for, she loved, she protected, and then she learned to say goodbye with pain in her heart. This, in her mind, was a part of life, and she accepted it. Life is what you make of it, she believed. It is this firm belief that enabled her to survive.

# 2

# SACRIFICE AND PERSEVERANCE PAY OFF IN BIG WAYS

While Grandmother Beatriz and my Aunt Isaura bonded through the struggles of life, they also had many happy moments. Even working and singing together brought them joy and happiness. After Carmelita's painful parting, life was a bit more forgiving. Grandma Beatriz gave birth to two more girls! María Magdalena Gallardo Cortéz was born on July 22, 1950, and then, my mother joined exactly three years later on July 22, 1953. At this point, I introduce you to the pioneer of this book, and no, that was not Grandmother Beatriz, although she was an admirable woman indeed.

The pioneer I refer to is my mother, María Sandra Gallardo Cortéz. By this time, Grandmother Beatriz had either mastered caretaking when her children were sick or was plain lucky that she did not lose any of her other children to measles or any other virus. She and her three daughters became a team unified by love and a strong desire to survive. While Grandmother worked, the three girls helped and learned by her side. She taught them everything she knew. They became experts at housecleaning, doing laundry, ironing, and several other essential tasks. Grandmother became better at sewing, and was able to sew on a manual, slow machine she had received as a hand-me-down from one of the ladies whose homes she cleaned. This is how she was able to enroll her girls in school. She bought their books and school supplies with the minimal funds she had, and she made their school uniforms by hand.

As you noticed, Grandmother Beatriz gave the same first name to all of her daughters. In prayer and faith for survival, she named them María, after the blessed Virgin Mary. She had Virgin Mary's candle burning bright in her home and prayed each day for hardships to become easier to handle, and they did. She and the girls worked together all around the neighborhood, cleaning homes and helping with whatever tasks they were assigned. In the years that followed, Grandmother Beatriz and Grandfather Benjamin had four more children. Jorge, María Marta, Servando, and María Cecilia were born in that same home in Mexico.

My grandparents managed to make a life in the tiny home they rented. At this time, that one-room home had a tiny grill, which is what they used as a cooking stove, in one corner of the room. The other corners each had a bed or a mattress on the floor. On the main bed, a full-size bed, my grandmother slept with her two younger daughters. At times, they had to make space for my grandfather, when he was around. My mom and her older sister, Isaura, slept on a mattress resting on the floor in another corner. In another corner, the two boys took the last mattress on the floor, and my aunt Magdalena slept on a cot in the middle of the room. When that cot was not in the middle of the room, they replaced that area with a small table and two chairs they used for eating their meals.

My mom loved her early life in Mexico. They lived in Colonia Euzkadi and she greatly enjoyed playing in the backyard with her friends and neighbors. They had a big pile of dirt for competitive marble tournaments, and they invented other games that had them running around constantly. Freeze tag and hopscotch were two of her favorite games. She went to school by day, helped at home after school, then played in the evening into the late hours of the night, and did it all over again the next day. Her life was complete. She had all that they needed—each other in good health. She learned skills from her mom and her sisters. Magdalena had secured a job after learning a new skill—hair cutting and styling! With these skills she was able to help her family with the groceries and other essentials. She later taught my mom how to do it herself. Mom was thrilled to pick up new skills! She loved cutting hair, and she became very good at it.

During weekends, Mom and her sisters would help Grandmother with her house cleaning duties. Mom loved to pass the time as she did these chores singing lovely songs she learned from listening to the radio. She had a beautiful and powerful voice. She sang at every opportunity she got, whether it was at friends' or neighbors' parties, at group gatherings, or while she scrubbed her hands on the washboard while washing clothes for hours at a time. She even sang during playtime. She climbed trees and sang from up above to surprise any passersby. During one of these singing days, while washing clothes at a neighbor's house, the owner of that home approached my grandmother and asked her if she had ever considered having Mom perform for money. He admired her talent and told Grandmother that he could help her get started at nearby restaurants or other public places. My grandmother vehemently refused even the thought of that idea. There she was, raising seven children practically on her own because her own husband was a musician whom she rarely saw and whose money went to who knows where. That's the life that Grandmother associated with any singing career. She was not going to throw her daughter into that life; therefore the answer was a resounding "no way!" and that was the end of that. Mom did have other plans for herself, though. She had learned hairstyling skills from her older sister, Magdalena. At the young age of twelve, mom dropped out of school to help Grandmother Beatriz and her family by working full time. She was only in sixth grade, but she felt responsible enough to make a living and provide whatever assistance she could to her mother and siblings.

She became an excellent hairstylist. Mom worked in a hair salon named Salon de Belleza Alba in Matamoros, Tamaulipas. She learned everything about hairstyles and haircuts, and other useful stylist skills. Being able to focus on her job full time gave her a great sense of satisfaction because she was able to provide for her family. Grandmother Beatriz was extremely proud of her and her other two daughters. She was heartbroken by the fact that my mother could no longer be enrolled in school, but she knew that it was a sacrifice for the benefit of the family. Grandmother Beatriz had decided to sacrifice the formal education of her three older daughters for the sake of her four younger children. The two older sisters had also dropped out of school at a very early age. Isaura had only completed third grade. My grandmother was not able to afford her schooling in those early years; therefore, she had her work when she was nine years old. My Aunt Magdalena and Mom had barely completed their elementary education.

They had a lot to learn, but now they would be learning about life through full immersion in real life. They found comfort in that. Mom fully immersed herself in learning about life, about sacrifice, and about working hard to make a living—truly make a living. Grandmother Beatriz knew that this was a major sacrifice for her three older daughters, but her mind rested in peace in knowing that her four younger children would not only complete their high school education, but she would also encourage them to go to college and establish careers for themselves. Therefore, Isaura, Magdalena, and Sandra, my mom, had to work to save up enough money to send their younger siblings to school and eventually college.

Mom thrived in learning new skills, trying new things, and talking to people at the beauty salon. Then one day on their walk home from the salon with her sister Magdalena, my mom saw an electric sewing machine in the window of a fabric store. It was at that point that Mom had a great idea; she knew that learning new skills made them useful. She knew that's how they were surviving in the tough world that they lived in. Mom was not one to play the victim card nor to mope around about the life they lived. Mom thought they had a beautiful life, and they were healthy. They were together and they had jobs. This was an awesome feeling for her. She set a goal in her mind to make enough money to buy that sewing machine for my grandmother. She was not about to let it go to chance, so she walked right into the store, talked to the salesperson, and gave enough money to put the machine on a layaway plan. She was on a mission to make her mother proud and get her the gift that she'd always wanted: a shiny electric sewing machine like the ones that Grandmother had seen in the various homes where she worked.

My mom worked long hours, and she took as many overtime shifts as she could to save up for her sewing machine. She had so much fun working for that sewing machine, and it amazed her when one day she walked into the store and she was able to pay for it in full. She had done it! She finally paid off the sewing machine that she had been working to pay off for the last six months! Even to this day, she says often, with tears in her eyes, "I remember that day as if it were yesterday!" The store personnel helped her load it into one of her friend's trucks. She had recruited two of her friends from the beauty salon to help her load and unload it at their humble home. She recalls with enthusiasm the challenge that they had as they arrived at her home. If you recall the layout of their one-room home, every corner of their humble abode was already taken. There was a full-size bed for my grandparents and two of the children. There was a mattress on the floor in two other corners of the room, and one tiny corner of the room had turned into a tiny kitchen with just the portable grill. It was time to rearrange their home layout. They put all the mattresses up against the bed on one half of the room and the sewing machine with a chair and table next to it were on the opposite side of the room. The grill or kitchen area was left in the same corner of the room, and the center of the room remained for the rotating cot by night and eating table and two chairs by day.

My mother was ecstatic with their new layout design, and she was absolutely thrilled when she surprised my grandmother. Grandmother Beatriz walked into their home from a long ten-hour day of work and saw my mother standing in front of a large bulky item she had covered with a bed sheet. She smiled proudly and then asked her mother, "Are you ready for this, Mami? We've earned it together." Then she put her hand on the sheet and unveiled the shiny black Singer sewing machine for my grandmother. Both of their eyes filled with tears of joy. Grandmother Beatriz embraced Mom with such a tender warm hug that, in my mom's mind, lasted for an eternity. Somehow, they both knew that this was a real turning point for them and their lifestyle. My grandmother would now be able to take on higher-complexity sewing jobs and sew full clothing or curtain items to sell to her friends and neighbors in the area. They both felt a huge sense of accomplishment. Their life was quickly shifting into a better tomorrow and a brighter future for not only the two of them but their entire family of nine. They grew in faith and happiness. Life was good.

## SACRIFICE AND PERSEVERANCE PAY OFF IN BIG WAYS—REFLECTIONS

In this chapter, we reflect not only on my grandmother's, but all her daughters', **hard work ethic**. They were determined to make a living for themselves and ensure that their entire family was taken care of. Grandmother Beatriz was also **determined** to provide a higher education to at least some of her children, as finances would allow.

This required **sacrifice**, not only on her part, but also on that of her three eldest daughters. She pulled them out of school at a young age to work full time and earn enough money to put their younger siblings through primary and secondary school. Two of them were even able to earn a college education. Servando, the youngest, became a primary school teacher, and Jorge, the oldest of the boys, became a banker. My grandmother's and mom's hearts were filled with joy when they saw their successful accomplishment of providing an education for the younger ones to be able to help themselves and their entire family.

The strong sense of **family unity** and **togetherness** prevailed during all the hardships of my grandmother's immediate family. They each **persevered** through whatever obstacles came in front of them, and they gained tremendous personal satisfaction from helping each other out. This was something that I always admired in all of them. They lived a simple and hardworking life every single day in order to survive in their hometown of Matamoros, Tamaulipas, Mexico. They were proof that **sacrifice** and **perseverance** paid off in big ways.

# 3

# FACE YOUR FEARS WITH COURAGE AND HOPE

As a teenager, Sandra was an adventurous young lady. She was fearless and outgoing. During her younger years, when she was in fifth and part of her sixth grade year, she had learned to play volleyball. She was not able to join the school team in fifth grade, as the uniform was too expensive. When she entered the sixth grade, my aunt Magdalena, my aunt Isaura, and my grandmother were determined to earn enough money to buy some material so that my grandmother could make my mother's jersey for volleyball on the school team. The shorts were a special type; therefore they did have to save up enough money to buy her volleyball shorts and shoes. She was able to watch others play, and then came home to her humble dirt backyard to train and teach herself how to play the sport.

She taught herself how to spike a volleyball, how to serve it, and how to dig into the dirt to make sure it never hit the ground. She figured she had learned several skills through careful observation, and then tried these on her own. This is how she had learned how to clean homes, how to wash clothes, how to iron, and most importantly, how to become an excellent hairstylist. This enabled her to develop a fearless character. My mom would try anything. Did she fail and make mistakes? Absolutely. Many times, but one thing that I do know about this relentless warrior is that she never, ever gave up.

Dropping out of school at such a young age gave her a huge sense of responsibility. She knew that her family was counting on her, and she was not about to let them down, especially her mother. She knew many of the hardships that my grandmother had endured, and she was on a mission to ensure that life from here on out was better than those early years were for my dear grandmother in Mexico. In some ways she became a motherly figure to her younger siblings. She had to care for them, cook for them, and make sure that the outhouse had warm water for them whenever it was time for bathing. All these duties made her grow up fast as a teenager.

Sandra had tremendous passion for life, and she approached every aspect of what she did with high energy and enthusiasm. Due to her job as a hairstylist, she met many people, and she received numerous invitations to weddings and quinceañeras. Her customers enjoyed having her there in case they needed occasional touch-ups on either their hair or makeup. She loved going to these parties. She would not only make their hair beautiful and make sure that their makeup was perfect, but she would also make sure that she was well dressed for the occasion. My mom had beautiful, long, curly brown hair. She was five feet four inches tall, and she had a slender body that weighed about 110 pounds. My mom loved dancing. She was an excellent dancer. She could dance to all types of Latino music with great flare and impressive grace.

I'm not quite sure if it was her great looks, her beautiful hair and makeup, or her dance moves that one day got my father's attention at one of those weddings in Matamoros. My dad, by this time, had been living in Brownsville, Texas. My grandfather had secured a job with one of Brownsville's politicians, who had helped my grandfather process his citizenship paperwork. He had initially hired him to just do chores around the house and do his lawn maintenance. Over the years he realized that my grandfather had a lot more talent than to just tune up front and back yards. My grandfather learned how to build homes and got into the construction industry. With the money that he made in the construction business, he was able to not only process his paperwork, but he also got to process my uncle Hector's citizenship, and later, sure enough, he processed my dad's as well. My father, Lucio José Castro, was living on both sides of the border.

On weekdays, he lived with my grandfather in Brownsville, Texas, working at an auto parts store. During the weekends, he would spend that time with my grandmother and his five other siblings in Matamoros, Tamaulipas, Mexico. It was during one of those weekends that he attended a wedding in Matamoros, which happened to be the same wedding my mom was invited to. It was at this wedding, during one of those beautiful Mexican love songs, that my dad, Lucio José, asked my mom out to dance. Little did they know that this would be the start of many beautiful memories together over the next few decades. Mom was only fifteen years old at the time. Dad was twenty-three.

Mom's young age required them to have parental consent to marry. My grandmother had granted permission, and so on April 11, 1970, my parents, Lucio and Sandra, got married in Brownsville, Texas through the civil court, and their marriage was blessed by the church in Matamoros. Mom was sixteen at the time and Dad was twenty-four years old. They were a young couple in love trying to figure out the start of their lives together. Within nine months they were blessed with the birth of their first child, a daughter they named Sandra Lucila Castro. As is typical in the Mexican tradition, they wanted their firstborn to be a boy, so he could carry on the family name, they claimed.

However, much to their surprise, my sister was obviously a girl, a very beautiful, blue-eyed baby girl with honey-brown hair and pearl-colored skin. Although the blue eyes from two brown-eyed parents were rare, the blue gene was on both sides of the family. She weighed six pounds and fourteen ounces. She was named after both of my parents, Sandra, from my mom's middle name, and Lucila was a derivative of the name Lucio, my father's name. Sandra was born on East Jackson Street at a midwife's home. Her name was Yolanda. This home was just down the street from my grandparents' home, where Dad lived part of his week. It was literally less than a mile away from that home and less than two miles from the US-Mexico border. Obviously, they did this because in the future Mom and Dad planned to live in the US entirely, but for now they had to make do with what they could afford, and that meant living with my paternal grandmother on Calle Marina Nacional 7 y 8 No. 29 in the Colonia Buena Vista, Matamoros, Tamaulipas. Now there was Mom, just a young teenage girl herself with the birth of a baby girl at the age of seventeen.

Not long after that, just sixteen months later, I was born. Keep in mind that my parents were still very traditional Mexicans, and they still desperately wanted a boy. They were also quite unprepared to have one, and definitely not two babies. Whether due to lack of education or just poor planning, there I was coming out of Mom's womb at the same midwife's home just sixteen months after my sister's birth. There was a big difference though; my mother was in for a big surprise… literally! They had prayed and wished all nine months for a baby boy that looked just like my sister. Instead, there I was, a very bouncy and large baby girl. I am told that I had beautiful brown eyes and brown hair with chubby cheeks and rolls of skin on my thighs. I have actually tried to find records of my exact birth weight but have been unsuccessful. When I ask my mother, she says that it was clearly more than nine pounds, or at least that's what it felt like when she was experiencing a vaginal delivery on a midwife's hardwood floor. When I ask my dad, this kind hearted and loving father says that I was a very lovely baby girl who was born with a very healthy weight and good size. When I looked into my mother's eyes and asked her to please tell me exactly how much I weighed, she finally did confess that it was eight pounds and fifteen ounces. "But you felt like ten pounds!" she exclaimed. So, there you have it. I was a beautiful, brown, and round baby girl who weighed almost nine pounds. I'm sticking with my father's loving version, of course. I was not a boy, I did not have blue eyes, and yes, I was a bit large in comparison to my older sister.

To this day, my mother honestly explains how she cried when she held me. It's not that she did not love me, but she really wanted to give my dad the boy that they had been wanting for the last year and a half. Of course, this was not possible, obviously, and so she cried. She loved me, but in addition to the extreme amount of pain that my birth had caused her, she did say I was not exactly what they were expecting. We still joke about it. We laugh about my mother's youthful immaturity at the time and appreciate my father's loving nature. "This is the one that is going to give you many pleasant surprises in life," at least that's what my dear father would explain to my mom, who was in too much pain to even think of anything other than I was another girl and she clearly wanted a boy.

I also like to inquire about why it is that my sister has two names, named after Mom and Dad, and I only got Griselda as a first name and no middle name. The first explanation Mom gave me is that I was an "oops" baby. I was clearly unplanned as there is no way that such a young couple trying to make ends meet in the US or Mexico would even think of having another child as they got started with their married life. The other reason was that I was not the boy that Mom and Dad were hoping for. Well, lo and behold, there I was with just one name with a solid and truthful explanation as to why I only have a first name.

Mom now had two beautiful young toddlers to take care of while she was still a teenager needing caring and guidance herself. She was eighteen when I was born, and my father was twenty-six. My mother sure was growing up fast as a teenager, but she loved every bit of her life next to my dad, who was a remarkable loving husband and father who would give his life for his three girls.

## FACE YOUR FEARS WITH COURAGE AND HOPE—REFLECTIONS

As we reflect on Mother's life growing up fast as a teenager into adulthood, there are certain values that come to mind. One of them that I must point out is **honesty**. That is one attribute that I always appreciated and admired in my mother. She was always honest, brutally honest, even if the truth was not what one wanted to hear. That much I loved about that woman. She was honest, even when Dad pleaded with her to sugarcoat the story of my name and my birth. Another admirable quality is **courage**. Although I do describe my mother as fearless, as she would take on any challenge and make the best of it, there was, of course, a great sense of fear. There's still fear in her voice when she confesses that she was afraid to marry at such a young age, but she also knew that this was a positive thing for her situation. She knew that continuing life in Mexico with her family was going to be a continual struggle financially, so she faced her fears of pulling away from her family whom she adored and giving her life over to my dad. She knew that they would eventually move to the USA. This also scared her. She did not know anything about this new country. Her life had always been in Mexico. Now she had to eventually figure out how to be a wife and a mother of two girls, and live in a country that she knew nothing about. This took tremendous courage, but with **faith** and **hope**, my mother pressed on for the **love of her family**. She got married, she had her two daughters, and she was ready to take on whatever challenge was next. She was ready to **face her fears with courage and hope** with my dad by her side.

# 4

# IN PURSUIT OF THE AMERICAN DREAM

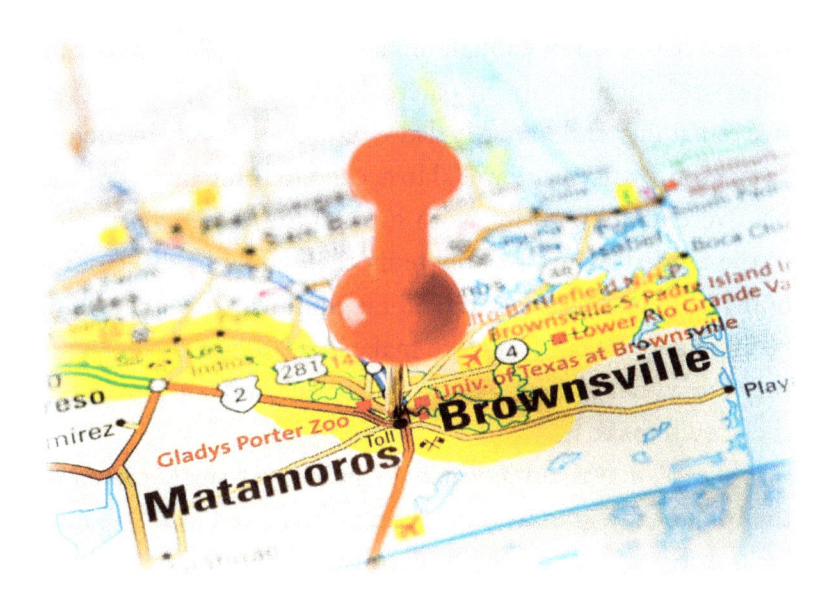

The weekdays seemed never ending for my poor mother, who was juggling her job as a hairstylist with raising two young girls. She had some help from her sisters and my grandmother, but ultimately the responsibility was hers. She had to reduce her working hours at the beauty salon, and with the money that my dad was making while living and working in the US, they were able to make ends meet. They did this for about a year, but this remote, distant marriage was a definite challenge. They had to do something different. They needed to do better, and they laid out a plan by which they would both come to live in the US. They would live with my grandfather, at his home.

At that time, it was not only Grandfather that lived in that small home in Brownsville, but it was his two sons, Dad and Uncle Hector. Over the course of about five or six years, he had worked hard to earn enough money to process the citizenship paperwork for not only my paternal grandmother, but for their five remaining children. My dad's immediate family needed to come to Brownsville as well. He needed to bring my mom and his two daughters to live with him, so they could start a life in the United States. Undoubtedly, that would be difficult for both, as they had been born and raised in Mexico. They knew nothing about what it took to make it in the States. However, they knew that if they planned things well and stuck together, they could make it.

The plan was for my dad to build two small rooms in the back of my grandparents' home. They lived on 2107 East Jackson Street, and in the back of that home there was large enough backyard space that my dad would be able to accommodate two rooms: one small kitchen area and one small bedroom. At the end of construction, it ended up being three rooms because there was also a tiny bathroom that was attached to those two rooms. That became Mom and Dad's first tiny home. It was really subdivided, or an attachment to my grandparents' home, but it worked. In essence, it was a definite upgrade from the one-bedroom home that my mother had lived in for her entire life. With some guidance from my grandfather and with his hard labor of love, my dad completed the two-and-a-half-room addition to Grandpa's home in about three months. The rooms, when finished, clearly looked like add-ons. The roof of the addition was lower than the main home. There was no connection between the two homes, just a dividing wall. That's how my dad wanted it. He wanted to make sure that his family was living separately from my grandparents' family, and so when I was a year old and my sister was two, we came to live on 2107 East Jackson Street.

Since it was just an add-on to the main home, we shared the same address, and we loved our little place. It had all that we needed. In the bedroom, Mom and Dad slept on the bed and my sister and I slept on the floor at night. During the day, that same bedroom was fixed up, by which I mean that the bed became a sofa, and it became a living room. The kitchen was a tiny kitchen, but it had all the essentials. It had a nice rectangular table with four chairs right next to a window. Mom made it a habit to always have fresh flowers on that table. Granted, they were wildflowers from the outside, but with resounding hues of yellow, orange, or purple. It had a small stove and one of those small portable refrigerators for our cold foods and a small sink for dishwashing. It was the perfect little kitchen for Mom and Dad. They loved making meals together in that humble little kitchen.

I think the bathroom addition was a last-minute idea because it was a very tiny bathroom with just a toilet and a shower stall. I do remember that the shower stall would get its water from the outside, so we went outside to turn on the hose water and that's what provided the running water for the showerhead. It was a nifty idea, we thought, and Dad made it work. Once again, a definite upgrade from the outhouse that Mom had been living with, where she used to go outside in the freezing cold and take a bucket of warm water to be able to sponge bathe herself. Now she had running water and a showerhead, with cold water, but so be it. We could warm it up in our tiny kitchen if we had to. The outside of our home was also very well adorned with nice plants, shrubbery, and this beautiful, tall orange tree in the backyard. It wasn't big oranges, it was tiny little oranges: *naranjitas*, we would call them. *Naranjitas* means little oranges. They were extremely sour, but delicious, and once my dad confirmed that they were safe to eat, oh boy, did my sister and I enjoy eating those tiny oranges every day during playtime! We'd come home and eat a bunch of little oranges. Mom eventually had to put a limit on this, for our stomachs' sake, but we still delighted in the pleasure of eating these tiny orange delicacies, our *naranjitas*, small and cute, like our home.

At this point I must confess that it was not all a perfect picture in our new place. There were some challenges, and although my sister and I were very young, the stories that my mom shared with us later in life really put things into perspective. We were essentially on my grandparents' land; it was their turf, and we were just renting from them. We utilized a tiny space in the back of their home, so we obviously had to pay rent. Since we lived there on their property, my grandfather made it a point to remind my parents daily that they should be grateful to him and that they should help him with anything and everything that he, my grandmother, or their immediate family needed in the home up front. My mom and dad always complied. They did their best to keep them happy, to make sure that everything that my grandpa wanted done would get done by day's end, and if that was not possible because my dad had to work, they would finish it by the weekend. Shortly after moving into that self-made home, my mom was able to get a job. This was her first job ever and she was thrilled about it! She obviously did not get to complete her education as she had only completed the fifth-grade level, but she was able to do odd jobs in maintenance. Her first job was at a restaurant called the Palmetto, where she helped clean the kitchen and dining area. This great restaurant sponsored my mom's citizenship. She was married to Dad, an American citizen, and she was supported by the Palmetto. Mom was off to a great start!

After her job at the Palmetto, Mom worked at a nursery where she cleaned and arranged plants outside. She worked there for a year under the scorching-hot sun or super cold winters. Later she was able to get a job at an electronics place called Carlingswitch. Honestly, Mom did not have any concept of what the American dream really meant other than she was happy in the States. She had a wonderful husband, she had two energetic and fun girls, and most importantly she had a job that could provide for her family's well-being. She was getting to know the area and, best of all, she was getting to figure out life in the USA. That brought her a tremendous sense of pride and satisfaction. Of course there were still struggles here and there, but both of them had jobs, they had a roof over their heads. They had each other, with two young girls to care for. My father had his job at the auto parts store as well. Both were working and life was good. They truly felt blessed. My sister and I were enrolled in a nearby elementary school called Longoria Elementary school. We got to make new friends in the neighborhood. We really enjoyed our neighborhood and being close to my grandmother just a few steps away. We loved spending time with our grandmother, Alicia, Dad's mom. She was such a caring and kindhearted woman. I think the fact that my grandfather wasn't all that nice to her was what made Grandmother Alicia seem even more angelic to us. She was the sweetest lady we had ever met. I still remember getting so mad during those times when we'd be at the dinner table at the main home and Grandfather would grab either bread or tortillas or something to throw at her to get her attention, because she was "not speedy enough" to get what he needed. Boy that got my sister and me so furious at our grandfather. I just felt like screaming, "Why don't you just go ahead and get it yourself?" But no, that's not what happened at my grandfather's home. We all just remained quiet, observed, and ate our food with appreciation and a bitten tongue. This was not our home; it was his and he reminded us of that every day.

After living in our tiny home for almost a year, Mom and Dad began thriving! From that day forward they worked hard and ensured that they did all that was asked of them, either at the electronics company or at the auto parts store where my dad worked. The fact that my grandfather made life a little bit difficult for them was beside the point. All in all, Mom did not have a stellar father figure of her own. If you recall, my grandfather on her side was rarely ever around. I'm not going to say that Grandfather Lucio Sr. was as bad as Mom's dad, but let's just say there were a lot of similarities between my two grandfathers. It was difficult for my mom to endure the demands of my grandfather's home and requests that he would ask of them to do day in and day out. After a while, this was getting to be extremely tiring for both, so life in the back of my grandparents' home did not last very long. Luckily for Mom and Dad, with both incomes providing for us, they were able to find and buy their first home in Brownsville, Texas. They were super excited when they were able to find a property about fifteen minutes away from Grandpa Lucio's home that they could call their own. With the money they were now making, they were able to save enough money to hire contractors to build their first home. This was our first home, and it was a very nice two-bedroom, two-bathroom, 768 square foot home on 544 Azucena Avenue, with a kitchen and a living room, and yes, the two bathrooms were fully functional!

## IN PURSUIT OF THE AMERICAN DREAM—REFLECTIONS

In this chapter we explore the concept of sincere **determination**, the willingness to **never give up** no matter how hard things got. That is true **resilience**. Even if life was not pleasant for my parents initially, they endured, they worked, and they smiled. They always made sure that, at least from our perspective, my sister's and mine, it seemed that life was perfect. In my adult years I learned that it wasn't so, but they loved their life. It worked for them, and they were going through those initial **sacrifices** to ensure that they made a better life for themselves. Their **hardworking nature** and **strong work ethic** also came through loud and clear. They both worked hard, and the reward was to be able to go on to a place that they could call their own. They were not thrilled with the situation initially, but they were **grateful** for it. That is another strong admirable quality that I learned from my parents, making sure that they sincerely **appreciated** anything that they were blessed with, even when the situation was not as perfect as they would like it to be. Another theme that you can gather from this chapter is that Mom and Dad were true **problem solvers**. Dad did not know how to build homes, but he would watch my father and my uncle do this and learned. That's not a skill that he possessed, but he **learned it** out of love because he wanted to build his own home. My mother was not an expert at any type of assembly process, much less electronics, but she learned it. She had **patience**. She tried, she practiced, and she became very good at it. That's what it takes to **pursue the American dream**. You never give up. You just figure out how to solve every problem that you confront and make the best of it.

> *"That's what it takes to pursue the American dream. You never give up."*

# PART TWO
## FROM THE RIO GRANDE VALLEY TO THE FARM

# 5

# A STRONG COMMUNITY MOVES FORWARD

Mom and Dad moved into their new home in 1975. The years that followed were absolutely amazing for all of us. Dad got a promotion at the auto parts store and now he was managing the place. Four years after living in our new home, they had my brother. Finally, a boy! They were ecstatic! Staying true to their Mexican traditions, they named him after my father: Lucio José Castro, Jr. Unfortunately, in Lucio's first year of life, he suffered a very serious illness due to a virus infection. He ended up in the hospital for several weeks. Mom and Dad spent days and nights at the hospital caring for him. During those long days and nights, we stayed with my grandmother Alicia. We knew something was up but we did not fully understand the seriousness of the situation. The doctors had told my parents that they had to prepare to let my brother go. He was paralyzed and unreactive, almost in a coma state, and they did not think he was going to make it. The only thing my parents and other family members could do at this time was pray for the best. By some miracle of God, after almost two months of being in the hospital, my brother Lucio finally came home fully recovered!

Mom had stopped working at Carlingswitch. She decided to dedicate herself full time to taking care of her three children. This was excellent for us as we got to enjoy quality time with her and she taught me and my sister how to cook, clean, and take care of each other. We even learned how to make flour tortillas and Mexican rice with my mom! In the appendix section of this book, I share with you my mom's recipe for these delicious flour tortillas and rice. My mom had become an expert assembly technician with her training at Carlingswitch, and after a year of being home with us, she secured a job at Atari, Inc. This was a very popular video game brand at the time. Atari was an American video game developer and home computer company that had been founded in 1972. It was a key player in the formation of the video arcade and the video game industry. Atari was top-of-the-line gaming, and she loved her job and the friendships that she made there. Everything around our home revolved around Atari: our clothing, and even some of our home decor. Our vacations were with Atari rewards and with Atari friends. We loved our Atari games. Pong, the most basic one, was our favorite. My sister and I would play that for hours. The other neat game was Asteroids. My sister and I were part of the Atari cool kids at Longoria Elementary, and we loved wearing our Atari jackets or T-shirts.

Atari was at the top of the video game industry for many years after its inception in 1972. It was a key player in the formation of the video arcade and video games. Its headquarters were based in Sunnyvale, California, or the center of Silicon Valley, which was the heart of the semiconductor industry. It had manufacturing locations in different parts of the United

States and Brownsville, Texas, happened to be one of them. The company began to face new competition heading into 1982. It made several poor decisions to try to maintain its leadership position, which hurt the company in the long term. One of the company's main mistakes was to venture into the home computer market with its first 8-bit computers, but there was intense competition in this space already. The company lost more than $530 million by mid-1983. That was the year that the Atari shock happened. As the leadership changed from one CEO to another, and as the incoming CEO tried to institute deep cost-cutting measures in an effort to turn around Atari's performance, massive layoffs happened throughout the country. This is when the shock of the Atari misfortunes hit our home in Brownsville, Texas. I still remember the exact day that my mother and many of her friends were walked out at once by the hundreds across the railroad that crossed the Atari parking lot on Jackson Street. This was a devastating day for many of us. Obviously, our family had enjoyed the many good tidings that were brought about by being employed by such a strong technology company. At the time, many of our school friends' parents were also employed by Atari. Suddenly, all that ended abruptly, and it was the talk of our school at Longoria Elementary.

I was in fifth grade at the time. I remember having extended talks with my friends about what could possibly have gone wrong, since it was such a strong company for many years. Of course, we did not understand the market dynamics or anything that was going on in Silicon Valley or around the world for that matter. However, we knew that our parents worked there, and we had a good life because of what the company provided, in salaries and in benefits to our parents and our families.

Now they had to figure out a new path forward. I remember having conversations with our friends during recess time at school. We wondered what we could possibly do to help our parents. Should we start working? Should we do more chores around the house to ease the anxiety of financial struggles? Eventually, we decided that we were too young to take on any responsibilities other than getting good grades in school. I remember that it was in those days of my fifth grade year that I started to develop a strong curiosity about the world of manufacturing. I was determined to study hard and learn a lot more about it throughout the rest of my years in school. If I was not old enough to help now, I sure was going to be old enough one day, and I was going to help the manufacturing industry to avoid massive layoffs like what the Atari company experienced in the shock of 1983.

Over the days that followed that shock wave of layoffs, I remember my parents getting together with many of their friends from the company that had also lost their jobs. We would get together for dinners and social gatherings. They would help each other out. They would give references to each other, and basically, the strong community came together to ensure that everyone that was looking for a job was able to get another job around the city. Their skills were extremely marketable, so it wasn't that difficult for them to find placement elsewhere. Many, like my mother, were excellent assembly and test technicians that were part of the video game industry. That was the hottest thing at the time, but no longer for Atari, as other competitors easily swallowed it up over the course of the next several years with more complex and graphically detailed games. In just a few short months, with everyone helping each other out, all those that were looking for employment did find other jobs. My mom decided to take another break from work for a short while. She and Dad were in heaven again. They were expecting their fourth child! I will not claim that this was a planned pregnancy, but they were extremely happy and waiting for what ended up being their second son. Emmanuel was born on May 3, 1984. As history would repeat itself, he was the second unplanned child and therefore only got a first name like me. He was simply Emmanuel, with no middle name. His name had special meaning though. After the health troubles they had gone through with my brother Lucio, the name Emmanuel meant "God be with us." That was my parents' way of praying and hoping that everything would be okay for their four children, especially this fourth and final one. Life at home was getting a bit of its normalcy back, and daily activities were not always as stressful anymore. That's what happens when a strong family and a united community move forward together.

## A STRONG COMMUNITY MOVES FORWARD—REFLECTIONS

The power of **faith** and **family unity** come to life. Certainly there were challenges in life, these are inevitable. There will always be tough times. How we **respond** to these challenging times is what matters most. In their case, my parents went through a very difficult time with my brother's illness, but they **stayed together** and **united the entire family** with faith and

**prayer**. Fortunately, they were blessed with a very positive outcome, but they were ready to accept God's will, whatever that may be.

"United we stand, divided we fall," was the famous quote by John Dickinson, known as a founding father of the United States of America and the penman of the revolution, although it can be traced back to the sixth century BC. These powerful words were later used by Patrick Henry, Winston Churchill, and Abraham Lincoln, among other popular figures in history. This motto captures a sense of **unity** and **collaboration** among a group of people. I like to refer to it as, "United we stand because we're all in this together," because that's what happened to us during that year following 1983. Many of the families, including mine, were struggling with financial burdens and were basically going through different levels of anxiety trying to figure out how to move forward past these massive layoffs and still pay their bills.

What these powerful words imply is that it takes a group of people coming **together** to make things happen. No one really accomplishes anything solely on their own. There's always someone there to help, to guide, to support, or to simply motivate you. In this case, during this very difficult time, not only for my parents, but for many families in that lower Rio Grande Valley region of Brownsville, Texas, they found a way to unite. They collaborated with each other and ultimately, they found their way back to their pursuit of the American dream. That's how a **strong community comes together** to move forward.

# 6
# ENGAGE OTHERS ON YOUR TRAIL

Since my parents had moved us across town, my sister and I were zoned to go to a different middle school than where most of our elementary school friends were zoned for. They were headed for Cummings Middle School while Sandra and I went to Faulk Middle School. Lucky for me, my sister got to explore that territory first as she was a year ahead of me. By the time I got to Faulk, I knew several of my sister's friends, and they introduced me to some of their siblings that were in my grade. I was headed into seventh grade as a new kid on the block, not overly thrilled about needing to make new friends and establish new relationships with teachers and staff, but that was my mission. I wanted to make the best out of my experience in middle school. First, I joined the pep squad. This was basically a cheering group for seventh graders, since only the eighth graders got to be on the cheerleading squad. I quickly learned during our very first practice that our cheering chants were practically a tryout session. I could tell that the sponsors were selecting the best performers to be the leaders and captains of the team, so I had my mind set on being one of those captains. I cheered loudly, and I paid attention to all the instructions that were given to us. I was determined to stand out, and sure enough, I was one of those captains by the end of that first practice. My sister was a cheerleader. She was already in eighth grade and was very proud that I was made a captain of their pep squad.

In that first year of middle school, I also realized that I greatly enjoyed math and science. English and other writing and reading classes were challenging for me. I was a native Spanish speaker and English was my second language, so I could absolutely speak it, but it took a lot of extra work and effort on my part to get it right. Plus, there were so many darn exceptions in that language that I found it extremely difficult to master. Math was very straightforward; it was black and white. There was an equation and there was a solution, and life was simple that way with rights and wrongs and not much in between. It is a beautiful universal language, I thought. I remember being so thrilled in my honors algebra class about completing a project. It was to set up a bulletin board with the Pythagorean theorem and present it in a way that was fun and caught people's attention. That was not something that Ms. Manzano, our algebra teacher, had asked me to do, but she was very happy that I took that on and that I brought others along with it. I loved engaging others in things that I found fun and educational, especially if they also found it interesting.

Later that same year, I joined the National Junior Honor Society, which is an organization that you have to be nominated for. Although I did not know exactly what that was, I was very happy to be recognized for such a prestigious club. I remember walking into the very first meeting in which we had to select officers for the organization. That was the first task at hand, and we had a small group discussion as to what positions were of interest to us. I opted to lead the group as president, and I gave a short speech with my reasons as to why I would be most suitable for that position. To my surprise, I came out of that meeting as the new president of the National Junior Honor Society. I was excited about that! I had another opportunity to influence others and help them through my academic skills.

My mission was to make this club that appeared to have a geeky reputation a fun club filled with people that cared about helping others learn. That's what we set out to do. With that mindset, it was easy to learn together and get good grades in our classes. We were having fun, we were learning, and we were helping each other out. I was engaging others on my mission, and they were actually enjoying it. At the end of that school year, we had our awards ceremony. My sister was proudly recognized academically as the top 5 percent of her eighth grade class. Then they started calling out all the honorary awards for the seventh grade. It was customary to present these in backward order, so you're the top 5 percent if you're the last ones to be called out to get your award. If you're some of the last names to be called, that means you're in the top 1 percent. Many names were called. I was getting nervous that my name was not coming up. Once again to my surprise, I did not know that my name would be the last one to be called. I somehow managed to get the top GPA in my seventh-grade class. At a very young age, I was learning about leadership and about serving others. And I was learning about how we could have fun in that process of helping each other out. I guess I could say that I had this middle school thing figured out. I loved middle school, and by eighth grade I had the highest GPA, I was on the cheerleading team, and I remained as president of the National Junior Honor Society.

At this point I must insert another important aspect of my middle school life, and that was my middle school sweetheart. Yes, there was a boy, and the story that involves this young man from my eighth-grade year carried on into my high school years. His nickname was TJ. He was on the football team, and I was a cheerleader. We had fun attending many of the middle school football games. We had friends around us, and there were many social activities that we did together. One of the great things I liked about TJ is that he was also very much into his studies. I'm not sure if it was because he was into it or he knew that I was and therefore he grew to enjoy his academic studies as well. What I did know is that we both liked to study together and attend football games; therefore in my mind, we were a good match. I remember speaking to my mom one time about him and letting her know that around that eighth-grade year there are a lot of relationships that get started among the young kids in school. We were teenagers and there were many romances in the air. I was happy that I had TJ, because this one guy that unexpectedly happened to be my boyfriend for many years to follow kept me away from all the craziness of breakups and relationships. It was just a steady relationship that allowed me to do my cheerleading sport, my academics, and my extracurricular activities, and he was a part of it all. There were many beautiful memories of dances, parties, social gatherings, and a lot of sports games. TJ played football and basketball, and our cheerleading training sponsor made sure that we cheered for every single one of those games. That made life extremely fun. I enjoyed not only watching these sports but also watching him play.

One very vivid memory that I have of my middle school years with TJ was one somber Tuesday morning on January 28, 1986. Through our studies, especially in history and even in our National Junior Honor Society, we had been following the amazing story of Mrs. Sharon Christa McAuliffe, the American teacher and astronaut from New Hampshire, who was about to go into space as a payload specialist. My friends and I were extremely proud that Mrs. McAuliffe was a woman and that she was to be the first teacher to orbit into space! That was impressive and super exciting! However, we all know how that story went. On that somber Tuesday morning on January 28, news resonated throughout the various classrooms about the Challenger incident. We were in class when it happened. It was 11:39 a.m. eastern time at Cape Canaveral, Florida when it happened. In Texas, it was 10:39 a.m., and within seconds, the news spread like wildfire throughout the entire school. By the time the lunch bell rang, there was a very somber setting throughout every hallway, inside every building, and even in the cafeteria. I remember finding TJ across the street in a nearby store where they had a small television and they were playing and replaying the explosion of the Space Shuttle Challenger. There we were watching it, holding each other among friends. We cried. We prayed. Then off we went back to our classes because we had to continue with our lives. We had to continue and, unfortunately for those seven amazing astronauts, their lives had abruptly ended.

Over the weeks that followed, I remember diving into what had happened during this incident. I did my own research with the help of some of my teachers. At that time there was a lot of misinformation. They mentioned the O-rings that were the main cause, and there were talks about NASA and Morton Thiokol and some of the management decisions that were made at the time. There were also some politics involved, with pressure from the government to make sure that the teacher went up into space, because we had committed to doing the study of Halley's Comet back then. We did not have as much information as we do now about the incident, but I do remember being fourteen years old, thinking about ethics and engineering and how critically important it was to make sure all issues were addressed. This was a matter of ethics, and obviously, of safety. It was a life-or-death situation.

My interest in the manufacturing industry and in engineering and ethics as to how we made or designed parts only magnified after that incident. I knew that I was going to do something with manufacturing and engineering. I think that's why my passion was so strong for the industrial engineering degree that I eventually pursued later in life. This was the only sad memory that I remember about our middle school years. The rest of my time at Faulk Middle School was absolute happiness. We danced. We studied together among friends. We helped each other out, and we made sure that everyone excelled at whatever it was that they were interested in. My life in middle school was complete. My favorite memory of middle school was at the awards night at the end of my eighth grade. At year end, they called out a recipient for an overall leadership and academic award. They called it the Manuel Machado Award. This was a prestigious award given to the top student in the entire school.

There was a huge bouquet of yellow flowers at the front of the room. When they called my name for that award, I watched the principal head toward that huge bouquet of flowers and give those to my mom. That was the most awesome feeling in the world, when I saw my mom's tears roll down her cheeks. Then I looked at my dad and he, too, had tears in his eyes. Of course, I couldn't help but to shed a few tears of joy. I remember that evening feeling such an immense sense of satisfaction watching their happy faces. After all the hardships that they had endured, I thought to myself: if this is all I have to do to see these happy faces on my parents, well, I know what I'm set out to do. I'm going to make my parents proud.

## ENGAGE OTHERS ON YOUR TRAIL—REFLECTIONS

In this section, we learned about **starting over** and how that doesn't have to be a burden at all. Many times, parents will either need to move for career reasons or jobs, and children just have to adjust and start over. That's just a part of life, so it's best to just **make the best of it**.

I often hear many teenagers complain about the need to go from one state to another or from one place to another. I understand how difficult it is for them because it is tough to start over in a new environment. I'm not debating that, but I will say that there's always a good reason for moving. If you're not the adults in the home then you just make it the easiest possible transition for everyone's sake, especially your own. Nothing positive is going to come out of moping and sulking at the fact that you must start life in a new place. I would also encourage people to **join clubs or activities** to make this transition easier. You must **find interest in those things that**

**you enjoy doing** and become a part of that and engage others along the way. That is how you **develop strong bonds** and **relationships** with others, when you have common interests. I bonded with my cheerleading squad buddies and with the National Junior Honor Society members. We became close friends, and we were making sure that those two clubs were respected, because cheerleading was a sport and the National Junior Honor Society was a fun club that helped others with their academics. It was not simply a geeky club. We had fun being a part of something, and we engaged others along the way.

Those would be my words of advice: **have fun** with all that it is that you are involved with. The other important aspect of life is **friendships**. You need friendships, especially at that age when so much is changing. You want to make sure that you have people that you **trust**, and you can talk to. Whether it's a relative or a parent or a sister or just a friend, you need someone that you can talk to about the ups and downs that will happen in life. At that age and the early teenage years, yes, boyfriend/girlfriend relationships are possible, or they may not be and that is totally okay. If they're there, then make sure that it's a **healthy bond** with someone that **respects** you and that **supports** you. It is important that you are there for each other to **encourage** them to be a better version of themselves. Friendships are an important part of making it through the many hardships that are going to come through life. You'll need a friend.

The other important theme in this section is the notion of **historical events**. Those will always happen at some point or another. Ensure that you are informed about what is going on and do your own research. Find out about these events and look at multiple news channels, because the media will twist a story in multiple directions depending on their biases. Make sure that you dig deep into what is occurring and what lessons either you or your organizations can take from those. There's always something there, so study historical events. **Be intellectually curious**. Finally, as you can also tell from this chapter, there's that **selfless** nature that I got from my father. My father was a very selfless man. He only cared for the happiness of everyone else around him, and somehow all those people made sure that my father had everything that he needed. I am delighted that I got that from him. It made me extremely happy to help others with their studies, with their clubs, with their cheers, or with anything. **Engage others on your trail.** Enjoy the sense of satisfaction that comes with working together.

# 7

# PERSIST WITH RELENTLESS PASSION

High school years at Porter High School were filled with fun activities. There was football, soccer, baseball, volleyball, basketball, and numerous other sports that allowed us to hang out and socialize with our friends throughout the year. As president of my class throughout my four years of high school, I got to lead the coordination of numerous events at school. We had dances and fundraising activities for the various clubs I joined. I was enrolled in several honors classes, and greatly enjoyed the challenge that those brought to our academic curriculum. As we traveled across town and visited other schools for either sporting events or club competitions, I observed that other schools had more advanced academic courses. They had these advanced placement courses that were even harder than the honors classes we had at Porter High School. When I inquired about these, I learned that other high schools in Brownsville had these courses that allowed them to take an exam and depending on the achieved score, they could obtain college credit! People referred to these advanced placement courses as AP courses, and our school on the south side of the valley did not have any of them.

I was intrigued by this. Why was it that other schools had several of these AP classes and we had none? As I investigated, I made it a point to ask my school principal about it. He referred me to our superintendent in the school district. I was given an option to transfer to one of these other schools, but how was I even going to get there? My sister, Sandra, and I had depended on the public school transportation buses since we had moved to our home in the south valley. There were no buses that would take us to any other school that was not the one we were zoned for. I told our superintendent that this was not possible, but that I could help him get an AP program started in our school. The response that I got was the most appalling and upsetting response I had ever heard throughout my entire school career. The superintendent basically told me that the reason Porter High School did not have AP courses was due to the prediction that our students at Porter High would not pass such exams, and therefore it would be a waste of their money. I understand most Porter High School students lived in poverty and that we lived in the region of Brownsville that was more financially distressed, but that did not mean that we were not hard workers and that we were not just as intelligent as our counterparts in the other more affluent schools.

I remember coming home and telling my mother about how that discussion put some fire in my belly. I was so hurt and upset about what I had just been told. She very calmly asked me, "So what are you going to do about that?" and just left me with that thought in mind. I don't think she even expected an answer, she just asked, looked at me, and walked away. The next morning, I walked into our physics teacher's classroom to explain what had happened. He was also our senior class sponsor. In his awesome helpful nature, Mr. García immediately offered to teach us the AP curriculum in his physics class. I was delighted to hear that! Granted, I will admit that physics was not my strongest suit, but at least we had one course that we could all take together, and I knew that Mr. García would ensure that at least some of us would pass this test.

Then I spoke to our calculus teacher, Mrs. Iyer. She was an awesome math teacher from India. Mrs. Iyer would dazzle us daily with her elegant and colorful saris. Each day, she would bring in a new sari—something golden, something silver, something red and beautiful. They were always different colors with very elegant embroidery. She would also take the time to explain to us what each of her saris represented and who they were gifted from or how she acquired that specific sari. We loved Mrs. Iyer's stories. When I told her about my discussion at the superintendent's office, she was also willing to teach us calculus. However, this was not something that we could take lightly, she warned me. It was not something that could only be done during class time Monday through Friday. We then started looking at other possibilities where we could do an hour of class time in the mornings before school started or after school. Based on the few students that showed interest in taking the AP calculus exam, we quickly learned that all of us were extremely busy with sports and club activities. Everyone's mornings and afternoons were taken with practices and meetings. Therefore, she gave me an assignment to go back to my senior class organization and ask if anyone would be interested in taking a Sunday morning calculus class at Porter High School. I just needed to get a few interested students and Mrs. Iyer was willing to give up her Sunday mornings to come and teach our class some calculus! I admired that woman and Mr. García for being the first two to step up and say, "I can help," totally as volunteers since the school did not give us any school funding for this.

I made a plea to many students in our senior class, and we were able to get over twenty-five students studying calculus together on Sundays. We would go to church with our families, and then after church our parents would drop us off at Porter High School. Mrs. Iyer would open the school, so we would do a minimum of two hours of calculus weekly. We did this for weeks throughout the year. Mrs. Iyer followed the AP curriculum to ensure that many of the students that were taking her Sunday class would be able to pass the exam with a score of at least a three or four. The highest possible score was a five. We all knew that this took extra effort on her part to not only plan for her regular calculus class throughout the year but also to plan for her extra Sunday class, just for us. That caring woman had a huge heart. She loved calculus and she taught it to us with such fun expressions on her face. It seemed as if she made all the integrals come to life on the chalkboard! Yes, we used chalkboards back then. There were no fancy digital boards nor dry-erase boards, just plain green boards and white chalk.

Our Sunday calculus class was filled with cheerleaders, football players, drama club members, many National Honor Society members, and many other students throughout our senior class. We were doing something together, and we were on a mission to prove our superintendent and the entire district wrong. Our students of Porter High School could indeed pass the AP exam and earn college credit, just like some of the other schools' students in Brownsville were doing.

Then it came time to sign up for the AP exams. All those students that were attending the Sunday calculus class regularly signed up for the calculus AP exam. By that time several students had been attending the physics AP class preparation with Mr. García, and by then we even had a world history AP class taught by Mr. Perry in the history department. Whether it was cheerleading practices in the afternoon or club meetings in the morning, I was not able to attend the physics preparation classes, but I sure did focus on my Sunday classes and I worked hard to ensure that I was learning everything that Mrs. Iyer was teaching us. Several students signed up for the physics AP exam and for world history. Almost all of us joked that we could easily place out of Spanish in college since that was our native language. Our goal was to take and pass at least one AP class and place out of Spanish. That's how we defined success.

I'll admit that we had a lot of fun learning calculus together over the weekend. We also had a lot of fun signing up for the exam and going through that whole process. It was a new adventure for us at Porter High School. We had never been through this, but we were doing it together and we found that extremely enjoyable. I do remember one of the news channels coming over to our school's Sunday class one day to ask about what it is that we were doing. We proudly stated that we were learning calculus with Mrs. Iyer so that we could take the AP exam and prove to the district that the students could pass this exam. That made the local news throughout Brownsville. Our parents were very proud of us, and we hadn't even taken the test yet! For sure we had learned a ton of calculus and integrals, and all kinds of neat equations and theorems that Mrs.

Iyer was teaching us. The proof of testing successfully was yet to come.

Finally, the days of testing were upon us. We all got together and showed up in groups to our AP exams. I remember doing a little prayer with my friend Angie, who was also excited about testing, and we even did some motivational cheering for each other. Then off we went to take our seats and take the test. I thought that would be the longest three hours of my life, but in fact three hours flew by! I had so much fun taking the test. I completed the entire thing. Of course, it did take the full three hours, but it felt like thirty minutes. I turned my test in and my friends did the same. Then we celebrated test completion with a lunch gathering. We talked about how we actually felt pretty good about the test, but of course we had to wait for the results to come in. Several weeks later results did come in, and many of us were thrilled! Out of the approximately twenty-five students that took the test, about half of them passed with threes and fours! We celebrated and cheered with Mrs. Iyer.

I scored a four and was so incredibly proud. I had managed to earn college credits before even going to college! I was very proud of our accomplishment. We immediately took our results to our principal, Mr. Ortiz, who then turned these over to the district, and lo and behold, the AP program at Porter High School was born in the spring of 1990! We were thrilled and celebrated cheerfully.

Not only did people pass the AP calculus exam, but some students had also taken the physics exam and scored a three or a four! Others even passed the AP world history exam! We were on a roll! None of this would have been possible without the caring volunteer nature of Mr. García, Mrs. Iyer, and Mr. Perry. We were forever grateful for them. They never got monetary compensation for this. They just got to see the proud smiles not only on the students' faces but also on parents' faces. They, too, had made the effort to take us to school after church to accomplish something special. They had helped us make it happen.

## PERSIST WITH RELENTLESS PASSION—REFLECTIONS

The lesson of this high school story is simple, just **never, ever give up**. Several people or organizations may try to bring you down on occasion. That just might happen, especially if you're part of a minority group—any minority group. I highly encourage you to use that to your advantage. **Do not be discouraged.** Do not let that bring you down. Instead, I urge you to **stand up for what you believe in** and fight. Let your **perseverance** and **determination** drive you to do what you think is right. **Trust** me, people will follow you in that march. They will **respect** you, and above all, you will have a lot of fun completing whatever task you set out to achieve. Numerous times I have heard, "Our children can't do this," or "Our girls cannot accomplish that," or "We don't have the socioeconomic means to achieve that." Please do not listen! With some effort and a lot of **heart,** you can **accomplish anything that you set**

> *"Let your perseverance and determination drive you to do what you think is right."*

**your mind to achieve.** That road may not be easy or simple. However, it is extremely rewarding. From that day forward at our high school, I welcomed the many times that our Porter High School students were put down, times when they were told that they could not achieve something. That **ignited** some powerful fire in our bellies, and we set forth on a **mission to prove them wrong.** You are more than able to accomplish whatever you set your mind to, **just go out there and do it.** It is only your **mindset** that matters.

# 8
# HELPFULNESS MATTERS

As I explored life through my high school career, I quickly realized I got great satisfaction from socializing with others and helping other people. It made me feel complete, satisfied, and happy. This was a characteristic I inherited from my father. He went out of his way to help other people, whether these were coworkers, family members, friends, or sometimes even total strangers. He would lend a helping hand with a smile. He would then explain to us how they would now be able to do whatever it is that they were trying to achieve on their own and we made that possible. At my young age, I was learning from him; therefore in my mind, he made that possible. To him it was always a "we." Our family was one unit and he constantly reminded us of that. One time I asked my dad why he went out of his way to help other people. His reply was powerful. He said, "*Mijita*," a Spanish endearment meaning "my little daughter," "I came to this country with nothing, but I had your mother and together we made something happen. We were never alone. There was always help and a caring hand there to guide us and help us. We just had to take advantage of this and appreciate the chances that came our way. Now it's time to pay it forward."

This stuck with me through my entire life. It was quite pronounced throughout my high school years, where I greatly enjoyed my academics and leading organizations. I was sought out for leadership roles. Over the four years of high school, I was class president. I was there to help my classmates accomplish whatever was on our minds. The senior class was an organization of camaraderie, of helpfulness, and of unity. We were working toward common goals and we had fun along the way. We worked hard through many fundraising activities. We washed many vehicles, we sold many food items, we had elaborate barbecue sales, and we ensured that our goals were always met. No matter how high we set our goals, we created detailed plans to achieve them.

For example, during our senior year, somebody called out the crazy idea of sending some students to Disney World for our end-of-the-year senior class trip. At first, we all chuckled. Then we all looked at each other and said, "Why not?" Off we went to orchestrate a plan to achieve the financial goal that was needed to send whoever signed up for this trip. At the end of our senior year, the class of 1990 of Porter High School from Brownsville, Texas, was navigating the sidewalks of Disney World in Orlando, Florida. This would not have been possible without the dedication of our senior class sponsor, Mr. García, who was also our physics teacher; our parents; and the extreme dedication and hard work of all the students that went on that trip. Another activity I greatly enjoyed was cheerleading. For those skeptics that claim cheerleading was not a sport, I firmly disagree with them. I was a cheerleader, and this was definitely a sport. When our cheerleading sponsor made us run miles before practice every day and then workout intensely with dance routines, pyramid climbs, artistic jumps, cheers, and chants, trust me, cheerleading is a sport. I greatly enjoyed the camaraderie that was made on our cheerleading squad. Adel, my best friend to this day, was our head cheerleader, and I was her assistant, a cohead cheerleader. Together, we ensured our team members were not only getting the exercise that we needed, but that we were cheering for every sport possible. If our schedule allowed it, and we had a bus to get there, we were there cheering for that team. We also had several cheerleading competitions throughout the year, many of which we won. We even qualified and competed at the Texas State Cheerleading Competition in our senior year.

Not everything was roses and rainbows though; we had a no pass, no play rule. I clearly remember how challenging that rule was for some of my teammates, as academic studies were not top of mind for everyone. As one of the leaders in the squad, it was my duty to support every partner in staying on the team. This meant we had to pass our classes, meaning earn a C or better in all our academic courses, otherwise we were disqualified from participating that semester. Because I greatly enjoyed studying, this came easy for me, but it was not that easy for my friends. This is not to discredit them, because they were hardworking, smart, and dedicated students, but every once in a while, there was a class or two they found challenging. I remember our freshman year, when the first reporting period ended and all of us were on the team. Then along came the second reporting period. That must have been a very tough one academically, because everyone except for me on the freshman cheerleading team got a D in at least one class. That was devastating for our freshman cheerleading squad! That meant that the entire team except for one was benched for a semester until grades improved. There I was, a single person on a team that obviously could not perform with just one cheerleader. For that one semester, I was moved up to the varsity squad! It was super exciting for me! Of course, I was sad that my friends on the freshman cheerleading squad were not there with me, but it was a great experience to cheer with the varsity team and learn from juniors and seniors at our school. They also seemed to appreciate having a youngling on their squad that they could toss around and boss around, but I enjoyed every bit of it. I even got to participate in football games where I was cheering with the varsity squad. I was a young cheerleader in this crowd of Porter High School Cowboy fans, cheering my lungs out with the older classmates. Those few weeks were quite memorable. That was an exciting time in my life. I helped my freshman cheerleading buddies study and come back to the squad so we could have our full team again. We had a darn good cheerleading squad, but without them we were zero.

That second semester was the only one in which my buddies failed the no pass, no play rule. After that, we all made a pledge to each other that we would study together, read on the bus on the way to games, work together, and do whatever was needed to ensure we were not disqualified from cheering again. Another concern arose that same year. Our football players also had to abide by the same rule, and we wanted to continue to enjoy our football games with a full team. Some of them struggled with some academics as well, and I remember approaching the coach about this topic. He expressed his concern about some of his football players who were benched because of the no pass, no play rule. We put our minds together and determined that we would ask some of our cheerleaders, my freshman class officers, and National Honor Society friends to tutor the football players before or after practice. He thought that was a great idea. Of course, the football players would greatly enjoy spending time with the cheerleaders, and they would probably listen to them more than their teachers. We did this for a period of several weeks. We had fun tutoring them to ensure they remained on the team and played their games for the school. Although it was a bit stinky in that study area, it was quite fun! We spent some time, upon the coach's request, tutoring and helping with their homework. Then after some study time, they continued studying on their own. We got that tutoring program started and that was extremely rewarding for all of us: the football players that were taking it, the cheerleaders, class officers, and National Honor Society members who volunteered, and, of course, the coach who got to keep his players.

These helpful events happened throughout the four years of high school. We succeeded together. There was a sense of friendship and togetherness that epitomized our high school class of 1990. There were side benefits to these experiences. First, my skills in math and science improved, which are subjects my friends needed most help with. Every time I helped someone with mathematical concepts, I was reinforcing the learning myself. I was not studying extensively; I was just having fun helping others. I loved learning new concepts at school, and I enjoyed reinforcing those teachings to others. I believe this is what helped me retain the valedictorian status throughout the four years of high school. I was at times called a nerd or a geek, but I loved learning and I love helping others with their academics, so I took the title proudly. I was a top nerd of my cheerleading squad who was there to help others when they needed a helping hand. That made me smile.

I think the fact that I reached out to help others even when they did not ask for it was why people appreciated my efforts. I did not expect anything in return, other than watching them succeed or watching them stay on the cheerleading team or watching them stay on the football field and master the no pass, no play rule. I represented the school in academic or other competitions. My senior year was filled with experiences, such as being selected as the school's homecoming queen. Our senior year both TJ and I were selected as homecoming king and queen. He was on the football team and I was on the cheerleading squad, and we both worked hard in our senior class to ensure that people were accomplishing their planned endeavors. I even got to go to Veracruz to represent our high school as the homecoming queen in a parade, and I got to participate in a homecoming queen pageant across the state of Texas. I did not do so well in the pageant, but I participated and met many other friendly ladies from other schools. In Veracruz, I was in a parade on a float with Miss Veracruz. I learned how to do proper hand-waving like what they teach you in modeling agencies. I remember her teaching me the hand, hand, elbow, elbow routine, but what I did not know is that you had to do that for hours at a time throughout the entire parade!

I kept thinking to myself, "Lady, I have no idea how you continue this, but it is extremely difficult to do. The action itself is simple, but to hold your arm up and wave it in that motion for hours at a time, not so easy." I was glad that I was only the homecoming queen of Brownsville Porter High School and not Miss Veracruz or Miss anything that had to endure this waving pain.

Nonetheless, it was an experience that I will always remember. Sometime during our senior year, TJ and I had normal couple struggles and we did end up breaking up. We had parted ways by the time prom came around. It was a surprise to me when our senior class would elect us as king and queen again, for the junior-senior prom this time. We were no longer a couple; therefore I figured they would not think of us as a couple representing the senior class. Well to our surprise, we were up on the stage during the prom announcements, and there I was crowned prom queen and TJ was elected prom king. We ended up going to the dance together, probably in hopes that we would get back together. I'm not sure if that was possible, but our senior class was clearly making a statement when they elected us. I went on to represent our class as the prom queen for the 1990 school year.

I believe this success came not from tirelessly campaigning and gathering votes, but from spending four years sincerely and authentically supporting other students. They had noticed and knew that it was not about wanting to get publicity for myself, but about helping them and making sure we were all working toward a common goal. We were achieving something together. That was sincerely appreciated, and I guess they expressed it in the votes that I received in these social elections. The final well-deserved accomplishment was graduating top of my class as the senior class valedictorian. I had studied my academic subjects repeatedly, so I easily secured the top spot of our graduating class. All in all, I greatly enjoyed my four years of high school. It was a "challenged school" in a region of Brownsville that was not the most affluent, but we worked hard, and we did things together. That's why we thrived at Porter High.

## HELPFULNESS MATTERS—REFLECTIONS

Nothing is achieved individually. I strongly believe that there's always some powerful **influence** that enables us to do certain things. There's some **motivation.** There's some **inspiration.** There's always someone there **advocating for your success.** However, there will also be those that are expecting and sometimes even hoping for you to fail. Our task is to have complete **awareness of our surroundings** and the influencing forces around us. Expert psychiatrists define these negative forces as common external and innate forces within our own minds. These are forces that tend to bring us down and are the easiest path forward. If you listen to these degrading forces, you will probably not accomplish what you set out to do. However, there are also **positive forces** within our innate personalities, and we must dig deep and find these positive forces because they are there. They help us **achieve whatever we set our minds to achieve.** That is what I chose to do. I also chose to help others to find their positive forces and capitalize on them. I did this because it was extremely gratifying inside. It filled me with warmth and happiness to see other people succeed and be a tiny part of their success. That was my happiness. I was finding things that were **more important than my own** endeavors and **dedicated** myself to them. I was fulfilling not only their needs but also making things extremely **gratifying** for myself. I think this is what true **helpfulness** is. It is that nature of supporting others whether they ask for it or not and making sure that they're moving in a positive direction with whatever challenge they're trying to overcome. As you conclude this chapter, I encourage you to reflect on that and see how it is that you can help someone else. You can make a difference, even if it's just for one or two people. You can help them with whatever it is that you think they might be struggling with and then reflect on what impact that has on you as well. My hope is that you will find that **helpfulness truly matters to the soul.**

# 9
# APPRECIATE YOUR ADVOCATES, ESPECIALLY THE TOUGH ONES

In 1990 I had concluded my high school career, and I was extremely happy with all that we had accomplished together during those four years. Now it was time to explore the big world around us. Our senior class had accomplished so much together. We were able to graduate 651 students. That was an accomplishment, as the average number of graduates was about five hundred in previous years. Gladys Porter High School later became Porter Early College High School and received its "met standards" rating by the Texas Education Agency in 2015. In recent statistics, its demographics included 83.1 percent at-risk students, meaning at risk of dropping out of school, and 94.6 percent students who are economically disadvantaged, with 43.7 percent classified as limited English proficiency. These were challenging statistics as a bordertown school that was constantly challenged by socioeconomic factors.

On the one hand, it made us stronger in character; on the other hand, it did force us to endure many hardships. For example, we did see several of our high school teammates pass away as they dove into challenging drug-related circumstances.

We also experienced a high teen pregnancy rate, but it was also rewarding to see pregnant teens walking down the graduation aisle. It was awesome that, regardless of the challenges they faced, even if it was in their plan to be a young mother, they were determined to graduate, and it was neat to watch them walking down the graduation aisle and get their diploma.

Together at Porter High, we started the AP program. We had excelled in our academics, and we had helped each other start different clubs and organizations that not only made a difference for our school, but for the community at large. Our graduating class of 1990 was able to send over thirty people out of state to either international universities, Ivy League schools, or other reputable academic institutions around the world. That was the highest number that had ever been accomplished in the history of Porter High School since its inauguration in 1974. Our principal, Mr. Ortiz, and our counselor, Mrs. Stewart, were extremely proud of us, and we were extremely thankful for all the hard work that they and our teachers had invested in making this happen. One of our graduating seniors got to go to Oxford in London and several of us got to go to some well-recognized schools like Brown University and Stanford University in the US. In this section of my book, I give personal insights as to how I ended up at Stanford along with my good friend Francisco (Paco). The two of us represented Porter High School in the 1990 incoming class of the Stanford Cardinal in Palo Alto, California.

I say two of us because two of us did end up going to Stanford; however only one of us, that is Paco, was extremely thrilled to receive his acceptance letter into Stanford. There were several things going on in my life at the time. TJ and I had broken up, and there were hopes of getting back together. Keep in mind, I was only eighteen at the time and very immature about where life would lead me. Most of my friends and TJ were going to schools surrounding the Rio Grande Valley or Brownsville area. I specifically had applied to Rice University, which was an excellent engineering school, and I was about to accept my offer to attend Rice, but Mrs. Stewart, my counselor, had asked me to pause until I received all notices back from all the schools I had applied to. I had not applied to many because they had hefty application fees, but one whose response I know she was anxiously awaiting was Stanford University. I still remember that day in early April when Stanford acceptance notices were distributed. I was called into Mrs. Stewart's office. I could tell that she had already spoken to Paco, the other student who had applied, and had received positive news because she had a big smile on her face. She then asked me to call home and said, "Stanford letters went out today, you should call home and see what's in your mailbox." I did as I was told and I called my mom at home from Mrs. Stewart's office. I asked Mom to get the mail and let me know if I had received a small envelope from Stanford, or if it was a large package from them.

I honestly had no idea what I was asking for, but I could tell that Mrs. Stewart knew exactly what she was inquiring about. If it was a large package, that meant that I was accepted. She and I patiently waited on the phone while Mother went outside, got the mail, and came back to the phone speaker. Mom picked up the phone and when I asked Mom, "*Mami, es un sobre normal o es un paquete grande de la Universidad de Stanford?*" (Translates into, "Mom, is it a normal envelope or is it a large packet from Stanford?"), her reply was immediate and I was still on the speakerphone when she said, "*Es un paquete grande.*" The loud scream that came out of Mrs. Stewart's voice was memorable! She had tears of joy and gave me the warmest hug I had ever received from her. I can still feel her warm embrace to this day. I remember that day perfectly, because her tears were clearly tears of joy. I also shed tears, but I also remember being afraid. I was scared and uncertain, so my tears were not joyful ones. For the last few weeks, I had my heart set on going to Rice University in Houston, Texas, just a short drive from home. Now my counselor and my mother were plotting to send me far, far away. That brought a sense of fear and a bit of panic to my mind. I did not feel ready for such a big move. I knew that the curriculum at Porter High School was not comparable to those of other institutions that had notably high national school rankings. Our school was not at the top of the academic scoring list across the nation. It had not even received its "met standards" rating from the Texas Education Agency. I did have very good test scores and excellent grades; however, I also knew that at Stanford almost everyone was a valedictorian and everybody had excellent test scores. Let's face it, it was also hundreds of miles away from home and I had never even visited the school. The only other location outside of the United States I had gone to was Matamoros, Mexico, but that was just fifteen or twenty minutes across the border to visit my grandmother and my relatives.

I sat in Mrs. Stewart's office with Mother still on the phone. Both of us were in tears and then I whispered to Mrs. Stewart, "I don't want to go." These words prompted a quick reaction from her and she immediately lost her groove and her smile. In her mind, I had worked so hard and the application process had been a bit strenuous, but I had completed it and now it was time to say, "Yes!" I will admit that I was not ready for that. I was not ready to go that far away from home into a whole new world that I had never explored. I didn't even go visit Stanford when most students go and check out schools with their parents. We had no money for that. I just saw cool pictures and I applied because I was encouraged to apply. Mrs. Stewart only spoke English and my mom spoke only Spanish, so let's just say that the conversation among the three of us depended on me. Mom asked, "*Que dijiste?*" (Translates into: "What did you say?") I simply replied with, "We'll talk about it at home, Mom. I'll see you later," and that was the end of our conversation. Mrs. Stewart was very respectful of my reaction and asked me to think about it before I made any decisions. She asked me to come and talk to her before I replied to either university.

That evening I went home and I spoke with my mother. If you recall from earlier chapters, my mother is not someone that can be persuaded easily. Once she sets her mind on something, she goes after it. I guess that's where my own perseverance comes from. Therefore, when she asked me about what happened in my counselor's office, I explained to her what had happened and what I had told her. She gave me this very pointed, blank stare as if I had two heads. She looked at me in silence for what must have been just a few seconds, but it felt like an eternity. Then she very calmly says, "You are going to Stanford." She knew that it was a world-famous institution with a strong reputation for academics, and that it only accepted well-rounded students with exemplary academic records. She said, "You're perfect for that university! Whether it's three hours away by car"—which was the distance to Rice University—"or three hours away by plane, you will still not be home, so it doesn't matter whether you're in Texas or California, you're still gone." This was coming from the same lady that cried an entire month every single day when my sister, Sandra, went away for college! My mother cried every day for about a month and I got to experience this. During those days, I told myself, "I'm going to go close to home and maybe come back every two weeks so that Mom is not sad." Well, little did I know, but that woman was going to send me way farther away than where my sister went! And she was actually happy about it!

I reminisced about those days when she desperately wanted me to be a boy, and did not even give me a middle name due to her carefree mishap. Now she wanted to send me as far away from home as possible, all the way to one side of the map by the Pacific Ocean. I recall at the tender age of eighteen thinking, did my mother not love me? Later in life, I learned that it was my mom's pure and unconditional love that enabled her to force me to accept my offer to enroll at Stanford. It was a need-blind school, so my parents' limited financial resources and my strong academic record secured me a full scholarship to the university. I would have to do some work-study, but at the end of the day Mom and Dad would not have to pay anything for my education. That was one of the main reasons my mother said I had to go. I knew in my heart that this was the right decision, but I was also scared. Nevertheless, before the response deadline, I accepted the offer to be part of the 1994

Stanford University graduating class. I'd be lying if I said that this was my decision. This was Mom's decision, and at the time I knew that it was the right one, but in my heart there was a bit of fear and trepidation. Regardless, I knew that a few short months later, in September, I was going to be on a plane headed to Palo Alto, California. Stanford University has been affectionately known as "The Farm" ever since it was established by founders Jane and Leland Stanford on their Palo Alto stock farm. Their founding grant decreed that a farm for instruction in agriculture should always be maintained on university lands. In the fall of 1990, I headed to The Farm.

Arriving in San Francisco on my trip out to Stanford was an absolute blast! I was on a plane without knowing anyone at all. That was my first time ever on a plane. Admittedly, I was nervous and excited at the same time. What followed from that point on was absolutely incredible. The Stanford orientation volunteer team went out of their way to make us feel extremely welcomed and appreciated. They had studied our biographies and even our pictures, so they knew exactly what we looked like. The group that was picking us up at our gate in the San Francisco airport decided to build a small pyramid with six people: three at the bottom, two in the middle, and one on top. They were calling out each of the incoming freshman's names as we exited the jet bridge. I remember hearing my name in a loud voice amid laughs and giggles.

As we entered the airport gate, after the jet bridge, we saw welcome signs with "Welcome to Stanford, Griselda!" There were other personalized signs as well. I did not realize that there were several of us on that plane that were part of the Stanford freshman entering class, but in a matter of ten minutes I knew all of them, because I saw their welcome signs and I heard the orientation volunteers greet everyone. After this, the activities got even better! Now we were recruited to go and give that special welcome to other incoming freshmen arriving at other gates at different times. We had so much fun across the entire San Francisco airport welcoming students. That was amazing!

Immediately after gathering everyone at the San Francisco airport, we boarded a shuttle and headed over to the Stanford campus. At that point, they had welcome drinks, appetizers, goodies, and lots of music. We mingled with every freshman that was arriving. This went on late into the night, and the next morning it was early to rise because there were more social activities planned. We also had to familiarize ourselves with the campus. We participated in a treasure hunt. I tried to get to know every corner of campus and the days that followed were just as exciting and entertaining! The entire first week was awesome. One of the most memorable moments was the 'Full Moon on the Quad' event, where we hung out at the Stanford quad and an upperclassman would give a welcoming kiss, just a peck on the cheek, to a freshman, so that was also fun and entertaining! After the event's welcoming kisses, then the Stanford marching band lit up the place with music and funky costumes! The weeklong social gatherings and celebrations were incredible! I had kept busy the entire week meeting people from around the world, going to different parts of the campus, getting to know professors and students, and of course, all that Stanford had to offer. There was one thing that I definitely missed. I forgot to call home. I had committed to Mom that I would call upon arrival to let her know that I had arrived okay. That was a big mistake.

I don't recall exactly when it was, but I do remember a request for me to visit the Stanford admissions office. They informed me that I had a phone call from home and that it seemed to be an emergency. A sense of worry came upon me immediately, and I picked up the phone. It was my nineteen-year-old sister, Sandra, calling me and letting me have it because I had failed to call Mom when I arrived on campus. I could explain about all the fun and the nonstop activities that we experienced on campus. I could let her know that it was a total blast and the best decision that Mom ever made for me, but at this point, none of that mattered. The bottom line was that I forgot to call home and Mom was worried sick. After a well-deserved scolding from Mom, and after a few tears, she said, "Well, how is it?" By that point, I just managed to say, "Mom, thank you. It's going to be an awesome four years at Stanford. I sincerely apologize for not calling home. I will call you again next week." Back then we did not have cell phones, so it was not easy for us to connect at the touch of a fingertip like it is today. I had an AT&T prepaid calling card, and sometimes I made collect calls home. I did not fail to call Mom after that instance. If I said I was calling in a week or two weeks, I was absolutely calling right on schedule. Needless to say, you only make the same mistake once.

My first year at Stanford was incredible. It was filled with pleasant surprises and sometimes cultural awareness moments. I had never left the Rio Grande Valley of Texas and absorbing everything that a reputable institution like Stanford had to offer was thrilling and exciting. One of the obvious things was the level of diversity that we were blessed with. My freshman roommate was Becky from Palm Springs,

California. Then I met Mireya, Alex, Jonathan, Christy, and Al. Then I ventured out beyond my Lagunita freshman dorm and met Lorena, Cheryl, and Jesus, and many other friends at the other dorms. I would love to say that my first year was a breeze, but that was not the case. As I expected, I was not as academically prepared as other students in my freshman class. I noticed this from the level of participation in classes, and the number of hours I had to study versus my friends' study times. To get good grades at Stanford, I had to study about three times longer to ensure that I completely understood concepts across my various classes.

I was also not a well-versed reader. My reading was slower than others and it was obvious. Finally, the last and main struggle that lasted throughout my entire freshman year was my Mexican accent and unique Spanglish language. I honestly had no idea what Spanglish meant until I arrived at Stanford. It was clear that I could not carry on a conversation in full English, nor could I conduct it in Spanish! It was a good mixture of both. In my mind, I was speaking perfect English, but when I looked at the puzzled faces of whomever I was trying to have a conversation with, that was clearly not the case. My dorm neighbor, Mireya, pointed out to me that I was practicing my own language and that it was very common in bilingual-speaking regions like Brownsville, Texas. Mireya was from Los Angeles, California, so she knew exactly what I was saying, and she also understood my struggles. Good thing that she was a helpful friend, because that girl made me practice one language versus the other for extended periods of time. I spoke hours of Spanish with Mireya in conversation so that I could practice my native language and then I spoke English with the rest of my friends during breakfast, lunch, dinner, and any other time possible.

I had made up my mind that I was going to master both languages. I had to practice constantly every chance I had. That's what I did. I practiced nonstop and I received feedback from my friends and a few trusted partners, like Mireya and Becky. They corrected me when I messed up and combined the two languages again. At times it was comical, but mostly it was frustrating for me. It was something that I had to think about daily and constantly. I was blessed that I had these friends to help me through those initial challenges. I could have very well just shut down and not spoken much, but I challenged myself to speak out loud. With my friends' help, I practiced public speaking. I had to master both languages, not only for the sake of good social gatherings and friendly understandings, but also for good academic performance. I had to write essays and read volumes of books. I had to improve my speed reading, and I had to improve my English writing skills.

By the end of my first quarter at Stanford, I was better at speaking pure English. I'm not going to say I was great at it, but I was practicing continually. I had developed good study habits and acknowledged the fact that I was going to have to study longer than my peers. I also joined in many fun activities: football games, dorm parties, social gatherings, and just about everything that Stanford had to offer. It was my social haven. Stanford classes start in early September, and the first quarter ends around the holidays, so we get to go home for Christmas. This was another memorable event. I was excited to come home to Brownsville for the very first time after my first quarter at Stanford. I had so much to share with my sister and my parents, and I was going to let them know that going there was the best decision ever. I had found a place that was welcoming, inviting, and filled with diverse perspectives, ideas, and amazing thought-provoking conversations.

I arrived at the Harlingen, Texas, airport, which is about an hour away from my hometown of Brownsville, Texas. I clearly expected my parents' excitement about my visit after my first quarter in college and to be there waiting for me at the airport. This was definitely not the case. I landed at my gate and there was nobody there for me. Then I went down the escalator and headed toward the baggage claim area thinking clearly they're probably over by that beautiful fountain that's at the entrance, but there was no one there. I headed over to baggage claim and picked up my bag. I waited there and then realized something must have happened. My parents were not at the airport to pick me up. As the nifty problem solver that I was, I gathered my AT&T prepaid calling card, went to the nearest pay phone, and dialed home.

My mother picked up the phone and with a cheerful voice said, "Hey, sweetheart, have you arrived yet?" I said, "Yes, Mom, I'm at the airport. Why are you still at home? Did you get mixed up with my flight arrival times?" Her response was memorable. She said, "No, I got your arrival time. I know you're there safe and sound, so just take a seat as you'll be waiting for us for a while. The Mexico versus Argentina soccer game is about to start, and your dad and I are going to sit here and watch it. Then we're going to go pick you up." Say what!!? Did I really just hear those words? Yes, that's exactly what she said, and then she ended the conversation with, "I hope you reflect on what you did to me when you first got to Stanford that first week. We'll see you soon, goodbye." Well there you have it. That was my mother's way of not only loving me, but also teaching me a lesson.

Boy, did I learn that lesson because, if you know soccer, those are very long games, so sure enough I grabbed a book, found a chair, and there I sat for what seemed hours and hours, waiting for my parents to pick me up at the airport. When they finally arrived hours later, there were cheers, tears, laughter, and hugs. My mother made sure she proved her point. I was never to forget about her, my family, or home ever again, and if I did, there were going to be some significant consequences. I love that woman. I would describe her as resilient, loving, and very fair. She and Dad instilled in us a strong work ethic. I was also aware that my mom was learning through us and the experiences that my siblings and I were blessed with.

After I returned to Stanford for the following quarter after Christmas, I distinctly recall this heartfelt phone conversation with my mom. She had a big surprise for me, but one that she had kept to herself until then. She told me how inspired she had been by her two daughters going off to college and doing so well that she, too, wanted to have her own high school graduation. After the award ceremony during my eighth grade year, when I received the Manuel Machado award, and after my high school graduation, she felt inspired to go back to school and get her graduate equivalency diploma (GED). She graduated at the same high school my sister and I graduated from: Porter High School. She had done it! She managed to work full time and study for her GED part time by going to evening school, and during my freshman year at Stanford, there she was: my mother was graduating with her high school diploma at Porter High School. We were extremely proud of her! She knew I was unable to attend her graduation as that required a plane ticket back home during my school finals and financially that was not feasible. I also had to complete my finals, so she just kept it a surprise until she showed me that beautiful picture of herself in her graduation attire getting her high school degree. I remember her saying, "If my girls can do this, I can too," and she did it. At the age of thirty-eight, with a full-time job and four children to watch after, my mom graduated with her GED in 1991.

The years that followed were unforgettable. I worked hard to get the best grades possible. I was a wizard at math, thanks to Mrs. Iyer back in high school, every other topic was a bit of a challenge for me. Through constant focus and dedication, and some motivational help from my roommate, Jackie, I managed to maintain a grade point average above a 3.0 throughout my time there. My parents' support was constant. They were not able to help with my studies or with financial resources, but they did what they could to help me get through. Although I had a scholarship for room, board, and tuition, I still had to buy my books and everyday living items. Books were not cheap at Stanford. I treasured every single one of them, and kept as many as I could. My parents had figured out a way to help me out financially while I attended Stanford. Both of them worked at the time; Dad worked full time at an auto parts store and Mom had part-time employment. In later years, I found my Stanford financial aid application from when I first applied. They had a combined annual income of $21,000. Although not a lot, Mom and Dad had skills! They had cooking skills! All of my relatives and many friends in

Brownsville loved my mom's tamales. A Spanish *tamal* is a traditional Mexican dish made of corn-based dough and filled with beef, chicken, or beans and steamed in a corn-husk wrap. In the appendix section of this book, I share with you a few of my mom's favorite recipes, including one for these delicious tamales! Mom and Dad had come up with an assembly line process that took two days to complete about thirty dozen tamales. First day was preparation of all ingredients, and day two was spreading the dough on the corn husks. Back then, each dozen sold for $5 to $6. Before the start of each quarter at Stanford, my parents would send me $150 from their tamales sales to buy books and toiletries. With this and my work-study earnings, I was able to buy books and essential items needed. All meals were included in my room-and-board plan.

My parents created beautiful memories from their sales of tamales. They worked together for hours in the kitchen with upbeat Spanish music playing in the background. At times, they invited other relatives to help speed up the process. I guess I can claim that many of my relatives helped me get through my years at Stanford. At the end of my sophomore year, I applied to an overseas study program in Santiago de Chile. I told my mom about the overseas program at Stanford and she encouraged me to apply. A few weeks later, I was notified that I had been selected to the program in Chile! I was thrilled, and a bit nervous. How was I going to get there? My mother had a plan. She always had a plan. That summer, not only did they make many dozens of tamales to sell, they also sold their home on Azucena Avenue. Many beautiful memories were created there, but it was time to go, Mom recalled. She noted that the high crime rate in that section of Brownsville made it an easy decision for them to sell. I was extremely grateful to my parents for all that they did for all of us. My siblings also enjoyed the same level of support and loving care. That was how we rolled, they said. We always supported each other. I had chosen to go to Chile during my last year at Stanford and take my final electives there. I mastered my Spanish speaking and writing skills and was forever thankful to my parents for making that part of my Stanford experience.

## APPRECIATE YOUR ADVOCATES, ESPECIALLY THE TOUGH ONES—REFLECTIONS

Life is filled with opportunities. They are all around us; we just have to **make a choice** to **take advantage of these opportunities**. It simply comes down to making the right choices. At times, this could be challenging or even fearful, but it is important to **find courage** deep within us. Whether it comes out of us naturally or someone nudges you over the edge, you must exploit the courage within you to explore new horizons and **appreciate those advocates** in your life that are challenging you because they care. You may think that you don't have what it takes to do a certain job or complete an education. I am here to tell you that you definitely have what it takes. You just have to put some **effort** and **hard work** into it. If you truly want to pursue something and you're **excitedly passionate** about it, you can accomplish it.

Once you embark on these new adventures with **courage** and a bit of **excitement**, you will find there's a whole new world out there ready to be explored. There are many **opportunities** in front of you waiting to be taken advantage of—you just have to take action and make things happen. I needed that gentle nudge from my mother and my high school counselor to go and explore life in California on my own. I am forever grateful to my mom for nudging me in that direction. It was one of the best decisions we ever made. Although she did send me out there, I ultimately had to get the courage to do whatever it took to complete my degree in industrial engineering at Stanford University. I will admit that it was not easy for me. I had to take two summer classes outside of Stanford in order to continue coursework in the engineering school, but there was a will to get an engineering degree from a top world-ranked institution. I had to creatively find a way to do that and I accomplished it. Similarly, my mother had been **inspired** by her surroundings and her daughters to go back to school. At one point, what she thought was impossible because she only had a sixth-grade education, turned into her reality. She had to work hard and learn the language and learn how to take tests. She did it! She had achieved her high school diploma. **Perseverance, determination,** lots of **hope,** and **making the right choices**—that's what it takes to achieve a state of happiness that fulfills you. This is a reminder that there will be obstacles in life, several of them actually. It is up to us to not perceive those as obstacles that will deter us from advancing. We should think of them as new opportunities to **find a new path forward** on the road less traveled.

> *"Perseverance, determination, lots of hope and making the right choices – that's what it takes to achieve a state of happiness that fulfills you."*

# PART THREE
## LIFE AFTER THE FARM

# 10

# LIFE IS NOT FAIR, MAKE THE BEST OF IT

The four years at Stanford University were filled with memories and friendships that will last a lifetime. My beloved place affectionately known as "The Farm" prepared me well for what was to come: life in the real world. Now this had been quite an adventure. Let's just call it a roller-coaster ride of learning adventures!

I graduated from Stanford in June of 1994. My parents had moved from the Border Apartments, where they resided after selling their home, to another apartment complex called Casa Grande Apartments. They were there until the end of 1994, because with my first job out of Stanford I was able to cosign on their loan for a lovely three-bedroom home on Alton Gloor in Brownsville, Texas. Mom still lives there today. My first job was at AlliedSignal Aerospace in Arizona, which later bought Honeywell International and kept their name, for marketing and branding reasons, as the Honeywell name had global recognition. I found a perfect place to practice my industrial engineering skills, and I had the most amazing boss, Bill. He was someone who continually challenged me to take on more responsibilities outside of my comfort zone. He also encouraged me and supported me along the way. It was easy to lead projects for Bill, as I always knew that he had my back, and for that, I was going to give him and the company my 110 percent every time. I enjoyed working on critical assignments in partnership with Japanese consultants who stretched me to no end. The company was called Shingijutsu. I learned a lot from my Japanese partners. Every challenge was an opportunity to learn.

From the successful transformation of our first manufacturing site in Tempe, Arizona, to the global deployment of lean practices around the world in what we called the Honeywell Operating System, I was having a blast implementing lean manufacturing practices worldwide. That led to more globalization and site optimization projects globally. I was greatly enjoying my work and my travels. At the time, I was single, so coming home for the weekends was not a problem for me. At the age of twenty-nine, I met someone special. It was someone with whom I thought I'd spend the rest of my life. At the turn of the millennium, on January 1, 2000, I married for the first time. He was an officer in the United States National Guard. Shortly after marriage, he was transferred to Roswell, New Mexico. I greatly enjoyed the small-town living in Roswell. I learned to golf, and worked, and hung out with a few friends in the area. I left my job at Honeywell to make the move to Roswell and got a job at Volvo's Nova Bus Company. They manufactured city buses, and I became their manufacturing engineering leader. When I was thirty years old, my beautiful daughter, Briana, was born in Roswell – with her alien buddies, we teased.

We had a blissful, short marriage that only lasted a few years. In November of 2005, we filed for divorce, and I moved to Albuquerque, New Mexico. I learned life doesn't always turn out exactly how you plan it. I tried my best to make this work. I was a young Catholic mom from the Rio Grande Valley, and based on my upbringing, I was not supposed to be divorced. After a heartfelt conversation with one of the deacons from my church, I knew it was the right decision to part ways, and so we did. That was an emotionally difficult situation that only made me stronger in heart and mind.

In Albuquerque, I worked for a company called Flowserve. My former boss at Honeywell had called me about a job leading two manufacturing facilities in New Mexico, and I jumped at the chance. The job required some travel to Phoenix, Arizona, and Vernon, California, and extensive travel between both New Mexico sites, but they were only an hour apart; one was in Santa Fe and the other one in Albuquerque. For this reason, I enrolled my dear Briana in La Petite Academy. It was a nationally recognized day care facility in which I could take Briana to any La Petite location in the country! It suited my needs perfectly as a single mother!

During the next four years, I worked at Flowserve in Albuquerque, and traveled to Santa Fe, Phoenix, Arizona, and Vernon, California. During my travel days, my little champ came with me. She got used to going to various La Petite Academy locations. She became a regular at the Santa Fe and Albuquerque locations, while she visited the California and Arizona locations a few times a year. I was determined to ensure that my daughter had everything she needed and that she traveled by my side. That is how I got through my few years of single motherhood. It was somewhat challenging, but life was not fair, so that is how I dealt with my situation at that time.

Briana grew to be a social butterfly as a result of these travels; therefore, I never had any regrets.

I knew I preferred to have a soulmate, someone to share my life with that would also be a father figure to my daughter. I prayed for many nights, and in August of 2006, I met my now husband, Greg Abousleman. Keep in mind, I was a career woman and single mother, and I had very little time for dating. The resourcefulness granted to me by my mother and grandmother kicked in, and I enrolled on Match.com online dating. It was a perfect solution for me. They did all the work via our profiles, and I just had to meet the short list of men that were sent to me online. Now that was efficiency in dating at its best!

I want to assure my readers that this was no easy decision for me. In fact, when asked about the most important decision in life, whether business or personal decisions, my response is clearly choosing your lifelong partner. That was on the top of my list. In my opinion, this is the most important decision in life, and we don't always get it right on the first try. If it is not your first try, there is a significant amount of reflection that should happen to ensure we apply any lessons learned to any future bond.. That is what I did. I reflected, and course-corrected, and now I happily enjoy a renewed family life with my soulmate and lifetime partner, Greg.

By this point, Greg and I were both in our mid thirties. He was also divorced and brought two kittens to the family. We both knew we wanted more children. Once again, life can be unfair, and it does not always go how you want it to. We married on October 6, 2007, and from that day forward, Briana, our two cats, Max and Boo, and I moved into our home in Albuquerque, New Mexico.

Before exchanging our vows, there were a few things Greg and I had to settle. First, we confirmed that both of us were avid Dallas Cowboys fans. Football had been a part of our lives and we wanted to keep it that way. I knew if I found someone that was not a fan of our "Castro Football Team," my entire set of thirty-eight first cousins would disown me. Second, and this one threw me for a loop, there was no prenup or anything like that, but Greg's family was involved in New Mexico politics. The one assurance he asked for is whether there were any indecent pictures of me on the internet! I couldn't believe what I was hearing, but nonetheless, I was glad he asked, blushed, and we moved forward when I confirmed that my Web record was absolutely clean. The final point we had to work out was my frequent work travels. I knew that my career life was not an easy one, and I had to ensure we both had a good understanding of what my global role as an executive at a Fortune 500 company entailed. Fortunately, he did not shy away from my extensive business travels. After a beautiful wedding at the foothills of the Sandia Mountains in New Mexico, Greg and I encountered our first challenge in life. we found ourselves unable to conceive a child.

The months that followed were filled with doctor appointments, visits to fertility specialists, and many disappointments. My ob-gyn worked with me to ensure I remained healthy and positive. We tracked menstrual cycles, temperatures, and ovulation days to ensure we used data to increase our chances of conception. After several short-term celebrations past day forty of my menstrual cycle, my heart would sink when my cycle kicked in at the fiftieth or even the sixtieth day. This happened three times. Our hopes were fading, but we kept on trying. During this time, for work-related reasons, we had to move to Phoenix, Arizona, and therefore we had to find a new fertility specialist and a new ob-gyn. It all felt like an ongoing nightmare. Greg and I had learned a lot about cycles and temperatures and had taken many pregnancy exams. Finally, shortly after Christmas 2008, Greg and I got the most beautiful Christmas present: a positive pregnancy test result! We were elated! We tracked it every week for several weeks. We shared the news only with our doctor, and she was thrilled for us as well.

Everything was progressing as expected, but we decided to hold off on sharing the news with our parents and extended families, as we had exhausted them with hope and misfortunes. We were in week eleven, and we planned to let them know after week twelve. We did everything possible to take care of our growing little one. Then on a bright, sunny day during a spring training baseball game in Phoenix, Arizona, we experienced one of the hardest days of our lives. During the game, I noticed some staining on my clothing. Greg rushed me to the closest urgent care, where it was confirmed that our little one was unable to hold on, and this tiny life had ended. The emotional heaviness that squeezed our hearts dry was devastating and hard to describe. We couldn't imagine what we had done wrong. We followed every detail of the doctor's orders. We were shaken, surprised, and deeply saddened by the news. It was time to gather our strength and move forward once again. We scheduled an appointment with our fertility specialist.

After taking the initial tests and preparations for assisted pregnancy, we immediately went back to our specialist to plan next steps. During one of the final steps, a urine test, the specialist sent me back to my ob-gyn. With anxiety and confusion, I did as instructed and the following day I was in my doctor's office. I gave her the test results from our fertility specialist, and she quickly informed me that we were expecting again! This is just weeks after we had been told that my body would not be able to conceive soon after our last painful miscarriage. Nonetheless, she confirmed this with additional testing, and after getting the results the next day, I was back in her office to address the issue she had found. My results showed that I was expecting, and that my body was not producing enough progesterone. My doctor was thrilled to have found the problem, and once she confirmed that we were once again expecting, AND that she had found the root cause of our problem, we were ecstatic! I was finally expecting and our baby was holding on!

Due to my late age—I was thirty-six at the time—and due to my multiple-miscarriage history, I was placed in a high-risk category. The silver lining on that was getting an ultrasound every week during the first trimester and every two weeks thereafter. I greatly looked forward to my Friday afternoons with my doctor. In week five, we heard a precious fast-paced heartbeat from our little one. God is great and He had taken care of us all along. Sure, we struggled, but those challenges brought Greg and me closer together, and we learned a lot about ourselves. We had a lot to look forward to in life.

My international travels continued, my career was blossoming, and I loved my job. I enjoyed leading presentations in the boardroom, and facilitating training sessions with a large bump on my belly. I loved every moment of it. I even had to ask for my doctor's permission to travel to China during week twenty-five of my pregnancy. I felt healthy, and I had to deliver on a critical joint venture project where I led teams from both companies. Permission was granted by my doctor, and I carefully executed my international duties while also taking care of my developing child.

On December 31, 2009, we were blessed with our first daughter, Gabriela María. She was our miracle baby that held on for dear life, literally. Sister Briana was happy to no longer be a single child. She was already nine years old, and she welcomed our newest family member with open arms and warm hugs.

We were delighted with our darling Gabriela. With lots of prayer, warm wishes, and an overdose of hope, our dream of having another child came true. I continued to travel, climb the corporate ladder, and perform my duties in my leadership roles. I felt fulfilled with my amazing husband and our little family. We moved back to Albuquerque, New Mexico, after Gabriela's birth. I reflected and thanked the Lord for the blessings in our life. We had worked hard, absolutely worked hard, and it was paying off. I had traversed from the Rio Grande Valley in Brownsville, Texas, to the boardrooms of Fortune 500 companies. I earned my way to positions of increasing scope and responsibilities. Greg's career was also taking off, as he led critical missions for the same company in Albuquerque, New Mexico. We both worked at Honeywell when we returned to New Mexico. We had decided that I would be the one to travel and take on executive roles, while he kept order in the home back in Albuquerque. This may not be the way most people arranged things, but it worked for us, and we were happy. Greg always supported my career, and I in turn ensured that his career desires were also met. His strong-willed personality and satisfaction in seeing a woman in the executive ranks were what made things work for us. He did not enjoy traveling nor the corporate environment at the time, so he'd tell me, "Better you than me."

## LIFE IS NOT FAIR, MAKE THE BEST OF IT—REFLECTIONS

Life does not always go as you plan. In fact, it rarely does! There are certain events in life that will take you by surprise. That is why it's called a roller coaster, or like my Greg likes to say, "Life is like a box of chocolates. You never know what you're gonna get." This is a popular quote from Tom Hanks in *Forrest Gump*, and it is entirely true. Neither of us wanted nor expected to be divorced, but it happened. We also did not expect to experience four miscarriages, with one being at a late stage of pregnancy, but that was our fate. Of course these events in life are heartbreaking. However, what mattered most was the **choices that we made** afterward. There was always a **silver lining** in our misfortunes. There were many **lessons learned**, and there was always **hope**. Each time we had a setback, we **chose to learn** from it, and move on with **courage**. Life will throw obstacles at you that are completely unexpected, some people say unfair even. Nobody ever claimed that life was a fair play. Life is not fair, it is about sacrifices, and **challenges in life are inevitable**. We must use them to **propel us** into greater things in life. Accepting them as setbacks is to accept defeat. There is nothing good that comes from feeling defeated and helpless. We need to accept the challenges of life, stay together in **unity** and prayer, if you believe in prayer, or anything that **motivates your spirit**, and make the best of it.

# 11

# WHEN LIFE HAPPENS, EMBRACE OPTIMISM

I chose the executive corporate path and Greg's encouragement and unconditional support made it possible for me. These corporate roles required an extreme amount of travel, but that was something that became a natural part of our lives. My sister joked that this was why our marriage remains strong. "It's always like a honeymoon for you two," she'd say.

Whether that was the case, or we simply found an awesome partner to share our lives with, we lived a blessed life. After my work in globalization strategies at Honeywell, I became good at optimizing manufacturing sites and closing non performing ones. That's what brought me to another role as a multisite leader at Flowserve Corporation. Then the same leader who recruited me there, Jeff, also vouched for me when a leader from GE named Dan asked me to partner with him to develop a business operating system at Ingersoll Rand. I joined on that mission with Dan and others, and we made that possible. This role led to other roles as vice president of several functions, mostly in global operations and in continuous improvement.

I had truly developed a passion and a skill in driving efficiency with operational excellence. My career life was filled with travels, boardroom meetings, and presentations to customers and executive leaders. I greatly enjoyed those duties and my global responsibilities. Surely there were ups and downs in career life, there always are. It's always a matter of rising tall when you get punched in the face or fall. That was what was instilled in me all my life. I had nothing to lose, as I came from humble beginnings. However, one bad move or a few misspoken words and you could lose everything. That was the corporate world, and I got accustomed to that.

> *"I had nothing to lose, as I came from humble beginnings. However, one bad move or a few misspoken words and you could lose everything."*

During my career lattice, I took on several roles with varying degrees of scope and responsibility. I enjoyed every one of them, and I learned a lot along the way. I learned about authenticity, situational awareness, company politics, networking relationships, and about how to engage employees to perform their best and to have fun doing so. At this same time, I was having fun with my growing family. In addition to the blessing of our little miracle Gabriela, just a few months later, we were blessed with a very pleasant surprise. We were expecting another child! It was a boy this time. After our conception struggles, we were unsure if this was possible, but obviously it was and we were thrilled. Everything progressed smoothly during the pregnancy. Our son was born on March 24, 2011. I was in charge of critical joint venture projects in China at the time. I was responsible for three brand-new sites for efficient manufacturing operations. I was leading the team, and they were counting on me to successfully design and lead the implementation of these sites.

It was during this time that Gregory was born. He was the most beautiful surprise. Everything about him was a surprise. He would not latch on for breastfeeding, he would not eat, and he was the smallest of my three children. Something was clearly different than the experience with Gabriela just a year before. Needless to say, the following weeks were filled with fear, anxiety, and constant worry. We were worried about the unknown. This is the beauty of life; it is a complete mystery, filled with surprises. Greg was right in claiming that we never knew what was next for us in life. We just had to embrace all its blessings with a positive attitude. There was a reason we got picked to have our boy with a one in 25,000 chance of being special. He was now in our hands and in our care. We embraced that blessing with love. Gregory was fed through IV tubes the first weeks of his life while they found a diagnosis. At three months old, he was diagnosed with a syndrome called Potocki-Lupski Syndrome (PTLS). It is a duplication of a section of chromosome 17, called dup17p11.2 in medical terms, and it affects one in 25,000 people worldwide. A comprehensive study about this condition was released in 2007 by Doctors Lorraine Potocki and James R. Lupski of Baylor College of Medicine. This was another unexpected twist in our lives. Not only did we have a child who refused to get his nutrition, but we also knew very little about his genetic condition, other than it happened "de novo." This meant it was not inherited, it just occurred at conception by chance, a one in 25,000 chance.

The months that followed were busy with several doctor appointments and plans for next steps. We worked with five therapists and nine specialist doctors to ensure Gregory was getting the proper care he needed. We also scheduled for a G-tube to be inserted in his tummy to ensure that he got the proper amount of nutrition in him. Unfortunately, that was not happening until another three months due to scheduling issues, so we had to find a way to feed him until then. My dear husband did his research and found that every human, especially a child, has survival instincts. Our bodies do everything possible in order to survive when under extreme stress. Using this concept is how he was able to feed him. He introduced the milk bottle to his mouth. For some reason that we will probably never understand, Gregory's extremely strong gag reflex would kick in. Greg insisted on him sucking the bottle, almost to the point of suffocation, and right after he turned blue and purple in the face, Gregory would suck his bottle and drink his milk, one to two ounces at a time.

This is how he managed to feed our dear Gregory in his first six months of life. It was one to two ounces about every two hours, for six months straight. Gregory became Greg's full-time focus. There was no way that I had the heart to feed him that way, therefore Greg did this every day at every single feeding. That's what it took for our dear boy to make it to his appointment for his G-tube insertion when he was six months old. Needless to say Greg was seriously exhausted by the end of these six months. We were extremely glad that he was finally going to be able to get his nutrition in a much less stressful way, a feeding tube.

This was one of those experiences in life that you do not plan for. Life just happens, and you solve problems, constantly, one day at a time, until you accomplish one solution, then the next, and the next. That's how we worked with Gregory. There was almost no literature or guidance on his condition, so we took it one day at a time, with extreme optimism and hope. Several doctors warned us that he may not be able to talk normally, or that he would struggle with physical movement, even walking. We did notice this. Gregory hated crawling and tummy time. He insisted on scooting on his butt everywhere he went. After a while this became comical. He became a speedy scooter on his booty. Eventually, he did learn to walk at eighteen months of age, and then at that age, his physical therapist still made him crawl, for brain and speech development reasons. The army of doctors and therapists that helped us with Gregory were fantastic. Although it was impossible for all to agree on a specific path forward, they did provide Greg and I with all the necessary information to make our own decisions about our son. Despite his challenges, we treated him like we did our daughter, and expected everything out of him that we did of her. He would imitate her as much as he could, and with this stretching of his capabilities, Gregory defied all the odds of what they expected of him as a PTLS child. He learned to walk and to talk in a slow and stuttery but understandable voice, and he even learned to eat. Over the years, Gregory mastered many other skills. He joined jiu jitsu at an early age to improve his confidence, self-esteem, and athletic skills. He also played soccer early on. In addition to cringing at any sight of food, some PTLS kids also suffered from hypotonia, or low muscle tone; therefore, a sport was always good for his strength and development. With the help and loving care of many doctors, nurses, teachers, relatives, and therapists across three different states, Gregory grew to be a strong boy filled with positivity. He eventually was able to remove his G-tube when he was eight years old, and by ten, he no longer needed the special care of specialists and therapists.

The year 2015 was another difficult year for me and my family with other unexpected surprises. I was at work at Ingersoll Rand's Club Car facility in Evans, Georgia. I was leading a Gemba walk, and I was being shadowed by an executive coach, Karen. She was observing me as a leader in action as we walked through and I coached my team on the improvement changes we had implemented there. It was an informative and productive walk and both Karen and I got a lot out of it. I was ready for my feedback, which I had asked Karen to provide for me in front of my team, during our team dinner that evening. I wanted to ensure they also heard the feedback and provided their insights on how I could serve them better.

What happened on my way to the restaurant threw me for a loop. I got a call from my sister that my dad had been diagnosed with stage IV cancer. For those of you fortunate enough to not know what this is, it's the terminal stage after the cancer has metastasized through different parts of the body. Upon arrival at the restaurant, I first spoke with Karen outside and let her know about the news I had just received. I was unable to hold back the tears while I spoke with her, but I gathered myself together and joined my team, who was waiting for me inside. Karen and I had agreed on full transparency. She would provide all feedback, positive and constructive, in front of my team so I could also get their perspectives. That was my choice. Well now, I also had to inform the team as to why I was a bit "offbeat" during our dinner. I felt the need to just get the bad news off my chest, and allow us to focus on Karen's insights about my leadership style. By this time, I had already booked my flight to see my family in Texas and that flight was the next day. I informed them and asked them to keep my family and me in their thoughts and prayers. I was headed into unknown territory in life once again. My dad was the first one in our entire family to be diagnosed with cancer. After sharing the news, we proceeded with our planned activities, and I learned about and absorbed Karen and my team's feedback. I was glad that it was prewritten, so my news would not have swayed it in any softer or gentler direction. It was an engaging conversation filled with compliments and constructive ideas on how to do even better. I welcomed it with sincere appreciation, and quickly applied their ideas.

The months that followed were intense. I arrived in Brownsville and my siblings were already at the hospital with Mom. Every word that was relayed to us about Dad's condition seemed so heavy with sadness and fear. My mom described it as a never-ending nightmare that she couldn't wake up from. It was real. This amazing father that had taught us so much about life, about caring for one another, and about putting others' needs before our own was now struggling. That selfless man now needed us to lift his spirits and fight this thing. That's what we chose to do. Dad chose to fight for any small chance at survival he had. My mom, siblings, and I tried everything for Dad. We tried treatment centers, various chemotherapy sessions, different hospitals, and lots of prayer. My dad did fight a lengthy battle given that he was diagnosed with stage IV.

I realized during that time that life was not to be controlled. It just happened. It was beautiful, and challenging at times, and filled with heartfelt lessons and love. We watched my parents suffer for months, and there was nothing we could do about it. All we could do was be there. We hugged, loved, prayed, and created many beautiful long-lasting memories together with Dad. Emmanuel was living in Dallas at the time, my sister lived in Albuquerque, I lived in North Carolina, and my brother Lucio was in Brownsville. We all took turns to ensure someone was always there with Mom and Dad helping with whatever we could. Mom was at his side every moment possible, and after a year and a half, we knew she was beat with exhaustion. There was a time when Mom called all of us together and told us that Dad wanted us home. He wanted a birthday party, Castro-style, he said. When we told my cousins, they all knew what that meant. It was an all-out costume party for my dad's birthday on October 22. He wanted all of us to be happy and in costume, and to have games, tacos, tequila, drinks, and cervezas. Most of the food and drinks my dad would not be able to enjoy, but he wanted us to enjoy it. In late October 2016, we had the most memorable and fun birthday party for my Dad. We had comedians, costume contests, games, and lots of family fun. Dad had wanted me to do his makeup as he had chosen to be Dracula. He said he picked this costume because cancer had drained lots of life out of him, and now he was ready to drain the blood out of it. I ensured that my daddy's Count Dracula makeup was perfect. He was a very handsome Dracula in full costume. Mom was a green witch, my sister was a Mexican character called La Chilindrina, along with my brother, who was her sidekick as El Chavo. I was Rey from Star Wars, and my brother Lucio chose to be Doñald Trump, who was running for the office of the president of the United States that year. We had a blast celebrating Daddy, and a few short weeks later, my daddy passed away on January 17, 2017. He left our world but made a lasting impact on every single one of us, including his nieces and nephews. We will remember him with loving thoughts, always.

## WHEN LIFE HAPPENS, EMBRACE OPTIMISM—REFLECTIONS

Life had to continue for the rest of us. We had **loved, laughed**, and spent a beautiful life together. I glanced at my two brothers, and saw in them the charm and beauty of my dad's loving and caring nature. They both had his personality, and I was assured that this bond of my dad's departure would bring us all even **closer together**. Our care and focus shifted to Mom. She had spent her entire life with Dad since she was fifteen. They shared many adventures and precious memories together. As I reflect on these adversities of life, these unpleasant surprises, I also realized that they're inevitable. We come to this world, and there's a start and an end, and when something ends, it only means that there's another chapter in life about to begin. This was the **optimism** that Dad had instilled in us, and his departure was no different. We needed to move on with **love, hope, and courage**. There are many things yet to accomplish, is what

> *"We come to this world, and there's a start and an end, and when something ends, it only means that there's another chapter in life about to begin."*

I'd hear him say from the heavens above. Our challenges with Gregory were also never-ending lessons. He and our daughter Gabriela taught us that anything was possible, even when it seemed far out of reach. Our lives were **blessed** with a beautiful blue-eyed girl, and a loving, hazel-eyed, charming boy. My confident Briana rounded all of us with her free spirit. That girl was full of life, energy, and adventures. All this to say that blessings are around us, around all of us. We need to **appreciate** them. There will also be down points in life. There must be, otherwise we would not be able to feel the true essence of the blessings around us. Always remember that these adversities in life are not for nothing, and they're not forever. Therefore, when life happens, **embrace optimism**. This could be loss of life, loss of job, or loss of anything. Life does go on, and when it ends for you or a special someone, rest in peace knowing that you've made a positive impact in some people's lives.

# 12
# IT'S A JOURNEY, NOT A DESTINATION

Like many people navigating their early career and finding themselves in a sea of uncertainty, I felt comfort and wisdom in my parents' guidance. They instilled in me the morals, principles, and values that shaped my character. They taught me that hard work and determination created a powerful force that was energizing! I admit that I had fear of the unknown and didn't always feel equipped to tackle the challenges I faced throughout my educational and corporate career.

I left for Stanford University feeling nervous and even a bit intimidated. I did not feel fully prepared to take on the rigor of that engineering curriculum, yet I persevered and encouraged my own mind to take on the challenge. I had many demographic statistics against me. I was a first generation daughter of immigrant parents with low socioeconomic status.

Early on, I did not benefit from the resources and financial benefits that other students across the nation enjoyed. I believe this is what made me strong-willed. I took chances because I had nothing to lose. Failure would only bring me back to where I began, so while it was intimidating, it was also deeply satisfying to take those risks and 'give things a try'. The more I tried, the more I learned. My confidence increased and with that, my competence across several technical areas also improved. I loved the world of industrial engineering and I used that passion to make people and processes better, to their advantage.

My first job out of Stanford University was a blessing in disguise. I interviewed with several companies in Silicon Valley. At the time, the New United Motor Manufacturing Inc. (NUMMI) plant was in Fremont, California. This was a joint venture between General Motors and Toyota and produced thousands of vehicles using lean manufacturing principles. Lean is a methodology in which you engage all team members to focus on customer requirements and work together to maximize value by eliminating redundancies and wasteful processes. I also interviewed with Sun Microsystems, which was a high volume producer of computer workstations, servers and software.

My parents' advice for choosing a job was straightforward: select the company closest to home in Brownsville, Texas. They didn't consider other factors, believing that my graduation alone meant I had already "achieved success". I was on a mission to accomplish something much greater and to make an impact on a global scale. I chose the aerospace industry as it was fraught with challenges in my field of study. I had learned methods and algorithms that worked well in high volume environments. I also learned from textbooks that these same principles worked well in low volume environments, but I was on a mission to test that theory. The aerospace industry was the harder path to success in my chosen field of study, and it was the path I chose. I joined AlliedSignal Aerospace in my first job out of Stanford which later became Honeywell

International when AlliedSignal acquired Honeywell and kept their name. It was one of the best decisions of my life.

As a loyal associate at Honeywell, I was able to partner with some of the toughest coaches and mentors in my industry. My supervisor hired Japanese consultants to turn around our operations and drive them towards continuous improvement. This significantly enhanced my skills as an industrial engineer and it challenged me in ways I had never imagined. I took on roles of increasing scope and responsibility and I frequently volunteered for the toughest projects.

I remained faithful to the perspective of 'I have nothing to lose,' so I kept building upon my learnings and stretching myself. Internally at Honeywell, we designed a certification process for lean practices. I became a Lean Master after several years of implementing these methods successfully in partnership with a company called Shingijutsu out of Japan. However, that road was not easy. I traveled the world implementing these efficient manufacturing principles. I learned about cultural differences by immersing myself directly into various cultures to completely transform how they manufactured our products. I presented our work and accomplishments across many boardroom conversations to ultimately convince our leadership team to implement these principles worldwide, across every single Honeywell facility. That was an exhilarating ride! I became so competent in transforming lean operations, that I was asked to lead the global transitions team. In this role, I was to evaluate manufacturing operations abroad and determine whether the sites had to be transformed or consolidated into other manufacturing facilities. I was fortunate to travel to many countries expanding my industrial engineering skill set.

For personal reasons, I found myself moving to Roswell, New Mexico. I was married at the turn of the millennium and after traveling extensively overseas and coming back home to Roswell, I had to part ways with my job in Phoenix, Arizona. This required me to travel Monday through Friday, then fly back to Albuquerque and wrap up with a 3 hour drive south to Roswell. I did this while I completed my projects, but the extensive travels eventually led me to accept a position with a bus company called Novabus, owned by Volvo in Roswell, New Mexico. My experiences continued to expand as I led the manufacturing group at Novabus. I greatly enjoyed my role, and it was in Roswell where I gave birth to my awesome daughter, Briana. After her birth, challenges became evident in my marriage and needless to say, our marriage did not survive these struggles.

My last supervisor at Honeywell recruited me to a company that he had joined called Flowserve. My initial assignment was to evaluate the two manufacturing operations sites in the state of New Mexico. We determined that it was best to optimize the Albuquerque Operations and to close the Santa Fe site. I stayed on as a multi-site leader at Flowserve for four years before I was asked to return to Honeywell to join the Global Strategy and Integration team. I accepted that role and continued to travel the world to optimize our operations and spread our lean methodology.

My purpose in mentioning this is two-fold. First, it's important for me to share that it was essential to accept tough challenging assignments in order to stretch my skills. The other reason I share this is because I think it's also important to note that I didn't always know exactly what I was getting into.

I simply knew that I had acquired certain skills that would advance my career and taking on overseas assignments would only advance my skills even further.

These assignments also challenged me personally as a working mother. I remarried and was always heartbroken each time that I would leave my husband and daughter behind while I completed overseas work. I traveled extensively during those days and my daughter grew up with her stepdad as her main parental figure. He was Mr. Mom and Dad to our dear Briana.

Although heartbreaking and exhausting, Greg and I made it work and formed a strong bond as we maneuvered through parenthood while building up both of our careers. I became a strong executive leader on the road, while Greg held down the fort at home. I was the boss at work leading cross-cultural teams at work, while Greg led his teams at work and formed a strong foundation at home. Greg was clearly the head of our household. I would return home and basically 'blend in' to whatever efficient processes and guidelines he had established. This environment worked for us.

I became the boss lady at work, and Greg was our Chief of Casa Abousleman. He mastered the art of day care centers while he worked, meal times when he was at home, bed times for our children and all that came in between all of those duties. I still recollect these days with admiration, as I believed I had the easier role. He had to juggle multiple roles, while I focused on mastering my executive roles and making a global impact with the companies I joined.

As an Operations and Continuous Improvement leader, at these companies, then Ingersoll Rand and L3Harris

Technologies, I got to work with many teams across 26 different countries. I greatly enjoyed all of the lessons in the workplace — the successes, the mistakes, the assignments, the people and everything that the corporate world had to offer. It was my career development playground for twenty-nine amazing years.

## IT'S A JOURNEY, NOT A DESTINATION—REFLECTIONS

I like to define my **career as a lattice**, and not a gradual climb to the top. Each assignment taught me new skills and experiences. I learned and stretched my **emotional intelligence**, my ability to **transform** businesses and my ability to develop strong networks around the world. Although many people may think that goals are easily pursued, journeys rarely ever go in a straightforward path. They have unexpected twists and turns that each carry a lesson to be learned. If I had to do it all over again, I would not change a thing. I have great respect for the many leaders that framed my career and **shaped my story**. I was challenged and am truly thankful for that. I can now reflect on the many great leaders that I learned from over the years. They taught me to be **authentic, compassionate**, driven and focused on achieving **impressive results**. I also learned a lot from the leaders that I chose to never emulate as I did not approve of their management practices. I am thankful that I got to experience a variety of leadership styles that each taught me how to navigate successfully through my career lattice including the boardroom.

Some words of advice I would share is to always **raise your hand with confidence** when asked to try something new and challenging. You may not have all the answers, but does anyone really have all the answers to everything? NO. It is a journey of learning from mistakes, failures, successes and the many environments that you immerse yourself into. Every experience brings a sense of wisdom, growth and expansion. In order to serve others and explore their full potential as well as yours, learn to **dive right in** and make that **excellence journey** your very own!

# 13
# LIFE IN THE BOARDROOM

Throughout my journey from the border to the boardroom, I have gained insightful perspectives and many powerful lessons from my experiences. There are several that stand out, framing my character and my nature as a leader. I want to share a few of those experiences as I believe they can help younger generations in navigating through the corporate world, especially in executive environments.

First, I want to focus on lessons that my dear father left with me before his parting. They were simple lessons, or words of wisdom and caution. He taught me to be vigilant and watchful of some people that may not always have my best interests in mind. Many people will help you get to that next step in your career, however, there may be times when people try to bring you down, for numerous reasons. You need to be able to spot these hurtful characters and take swift action towards your career progression. Dad had his own way of communicating this to me. He used his loving words of care and concern. I listened intently and learned.

The first challenge I encountered post-Stanford graduation was when I was assigned to lead the lean transformation of our model site in Tempe, Arizona at Honeywell. I was working with several Japanese consultants. I formed teams and led the training sessions in the boardroom to teach lean principles to our executive leaders and to our implementation team members. I was blessed to have a boss, Bill, who believed in me and knew that I was the right person for the job. In a way, I think initially Bill had more confidence in me than I had in myself.

What I felt in those early days of getting to know my consultant partners was that I was not well received by them. I probably will never know the exact reasons. I was getting started in my career as an industrial engineer and was determined to give it my best to ensure a successful and long-lasting lean transformation. I reflected on what could possibly be impacting their 'acceptance' of me as a leader. Several potential reasons dawned on me: I was a woman. I was Hispanic and to top that off, I was only 5 foot 2 inches tall.

I had read business articles and was aware of the 'typical' American business leader and let's face it, I did not embody those characteristics. Tall men are typically perceived as stronger and more capable to lead. Back in the early 1990's, the good ol' boy network was more prevalent. Well, I was not white, I was not tall, and I was not a man. I was a Hispanic woman, a strong one at that, so I was able to fully utilize and embrace my feminine superpowers to engage my team and partner with my consultants.

My team members and my boss proudly welcomed my leadership contributions; however, my strategic partners were not as welcoming. I clearly recall a situation in the boardroom as I was hosting a training session. While the trainer, a Japanese consultant, was teaching, I was asked a question by a confused attendee. I was in the middle of my brief explanation when I heard a super loud thump on the table. It was the lead consultant who was upset that I was not providing him with my full attention. I get it, I could have waited until a break period to explain to my student about the topic in question, however, he did not have to make such a loud and pronounced statement. I can accept that what I did was disrespectful, and I will also claim that his reaction was even more disrespectful. I felt embarrassed, apologetic and upset all at the same time. He exchanged several words in his language. The translator basically translated, 'Pay attention.' I smiled and said, "there was a lot more in there than just, 'Pay attention', but please do ask him to pause. It appears that one of our students is confused and others may be as well, so I'm going to explain further in my own language."

I was determined to take control of MY boardroom. I was determined to show him that I was in charge, and that if he was there it was because I selected them to lead this work for us, and ultimately, I paid his contract. From that point forward, it was smooth sailing. Not only did he see me take control of my event, but my boss also pointed out to him that I was in charge of this project, and that I had the 'D' – meaning the decision-making power for who we decided to engage with as our strategic partners. I did earn his respect and ultimately his trust over time. I was proud of myself and continued to ensure that I addressed my partners with confidence in all of our interactions.

There are other experiences that capture the essence of being a woman in a male-dominated environment, in a more comical way. Earlier, I mentioned my travels to China and other countries to spread our lean practices and develop joint ventures. During these assignments, I ensured that I 'dressed the part'. I was presenting in foreign boardrooms, and I wanted to portray knowledge and confidence along with my male counterparts and other leaders.

I recall a specific meeting in which we proposed a desired location for our new manufacturing facility. I had done all my customer segmentation analysis and had strong arguments for why we wanted to be in a specific province in China. That day, I was wearing an elegant light blue business pantsuit. During the session, which, by the way, tends to be much more relaxed than stateside meetings, I suddenly needed to use the bathroom. However, I chose to stay because I didn't want to be absent when I was needed in the boardroom. The discussions continued, and I was finally at a point where I could not wait any longer. I excused myself and headed towards the 'toilets' as they refer to them in China. Well, I was in for a big surprise at that location. I had been to business trips to China before, but this was the first time that I encountered a bathroom in which all toilets were Chinese-style toilets! That means they were all flush to the ground! There were no raised toilet seats. I was in a sudden panic. I did not know how to use the bathroom! I figured if I tried to lower my pants and squat, I'd surely get myself wet. I was not about to go into the boardroom with wet pants!

My problem-solving instincts kicked in and I quickly paged Susan, my Chinese team member who was always by my side during these Chinese trips. Yes, we used pagers back then. Susan quickly came to the restroom and asked what I needed. I told her I needed help! I needed to know how to use the flat toilet without getting my pants wet! She burst out laughing and then proceeded to 'show' me how I should approach this. She was graceful and tactical in her demonstration, but I still did not see how I could accomplish it successfully. Finally, I chose to remove my pants entirely and continued with the instructions Susan provided. Mission accomplished!

Now I had to get myself back in the meeting room and prepare for my big presentation! I rushed over, and they were waiting on me by this time. I found my way to the front of the room, and made a lighthearted joke about needing standard work (a lean manufacturing term that means having standardized and documented best practices for any process) to be able to utilize the toilet effectively. I used that moment to segue with a comment about how standard work was helpful in any environment, even in restrooms. They all laughed, and the meeting moved on. Not only did I nail the presentation, but their jovial spirits kicked in as I chose to 'break the ice' with a joke versus try to recover from my obvious delay. When in doubt, turn to humor. That was my strategy, and it worked.

I also had positive experiences as a woman in a global manufacturing world. I must say that women do have certain advantages in this environment. My feminine powers enable me a keen sense of compassion and high emotional awareness. This was helpful when I was leading a team in Bintan, Indonesia in a lean site design. Our challenge was to expand the site for increased volume coming to this location. The site design was essentially completed when I decided to gather input from the employees before we 'locked in' our site design and turned it over to the facilities crew to make it happen. During these discussions I learned that a chapel was an essential part of what they wanted to see in this new expansion. The employees had daily prayer time, and were exiting the facility to find a place to engage in prayer, which was unfortunate because it was usually hot and humid outside. We decided to go back to the drawing board. I asked my team to design a chapel in a section of the manufacturing site close to the production area. This simple change was one of the most impactful changes we made to the site's overall design. The people of Bintan felt heard, cared for, and understood. Those are some of the feminine powers that I brought to the table. I insisted on making this chapel a reality for them, and in return, the productivity of that place skyrocketed! This was a win-win for everyone.

The last example of feminine prowess I will share is the time I led multiple sites as a site leader. I moved to Albuquerque, NM to lead two different sites. One of them, in Santa Fe, ended up closing for cost benefits and strategic reasons. The Albuquerque site was a performance turnaround for me and my team. I came to this company and to this site with no continuous improvement team and no training curriculum, yet I had to transform a poor performing operation into a shining star. That's what I did.

I came up with the idea to build flashlights in lean fashion and create my own version of a lean simulation to teach my team members about lean flow, standard work, and the establishment of key performance indicators. After we successfully learned these principles, we used those same flashlights to 'shine the light' on those things that were broken or not functioning optimally across our site. We had fun doing this, and we were able to fix and improve many aspects of our facility. We transformed our operation from the 30% range in on-time performance to the 100% level. We started tracking quality performance, and we were able to improve it by over 60%.

Finally, we also had to significantly improve our safety record. Not only was this one of the worst records I had ever seen, but we also had two pending litigations due to our safety performance. I cared about my team, and I also knew that we had some potential drug users amongst them. This saddened me and concerned me as they were operating heavy machinery. I prefer to not elaborate on this, but I will say that my compassionate nature is what led me to make some bold decisions to eradicate this drug use problem. Shortly after a near-miss safety incident, I decided to not only test the person involved, but I decided to test my entire second shift, which is where the incident occurred. I knew I would lose several team members, but I also knew that they were endangering themselves and others, so I had to send a strong message throughout the site. I did lose several people during this random drug test, but it was the right move. I had a hunch, I acted on it tactfully, and the solution yielded not only a safer work environment, it also helped the pending litigation get settled. Now I will not credit this entirely to my feminine instincts, but I will say that they led me to 'care for my team and protect them' in whatever means I had within my power, and I did that inside and outside of the boardroom.

I led numerous key strategic projects for large corporations, gaining wisdom and character strength with each one. These efforts resulted in significant performance improvements, and I can proudly attribute over $1 billion in operating income savings to the work my teams and I spearheaded over the course of my corporate career. Achieving this milestone in 2023 was a major accomplishment for me. The most rewarding aspect was collaborating with teams around the world, forming friendships, networks, and long-lasting acquaintances along the way.

## LIFE IN THE BOARDROOM— REFLECTIONS

I speculate that many people will take these lessons learned as trivial or not as impactful. To me, they **shaped my character** in a profound way. I learned that my father was correct. There were not only one or two, but several people who did not advocate for my success and career progression. That was clear. Fortunately for me and for many women out there, there were many more that were **strong advocates** and that genuinely helped advance my career. I will also say that most of my staunch supporters were men. I mention this because I feel it is important to note my own definition of feminism.

To me, feminism is about **women advancing through results** and distinguished leadership styles. It is about **doing the right thing for people** and genuinely caring for a group of people working together to achieve a common vision. I do not see feminism as a God-given right to be given opportunities simply because I am a woman in today's world. I must earn my place in the executive ranks, and I have to ensure that I **perform to the best of my abilities** to stay there. If I do not add value to an organization, I do not belong there. It is as simple as that. I will say that I fully support women enjoying the basic civil rights that everyone is privileged with.

I know, as a previous Board Chair for the Women in Manufacturing National Association, that we still have a long way to go with the equality of women's rights. I also know from working in a male-dominated environment that this is not a simple journey. In the 1980's the percentage of women in leadership roles were in the teens. Through focused hard work, and many other programs that better prepare our strong women to take on leadership roles, whether in STEM related fields or other jobs, I have seen improvement to now over 30%. Admittedly, we **still have a long way to go**, but I don't want to discredit the many men and women out there that are doing their part to advance women in leadership roles, because the bottom line is, we need us. We need more women to **drive performance** and **productivity** in the world's economy, because that is what we do.

# 14
# IGNITE YOUR PASSION!

During this final chapter in my story of hope, courage, love, and turning adversity into advantages, I ask that you reflect on your own lives. I firmly believe that we each have a purpose in life and a story to share. I also know that many people do not engage in deep self-reflection to find that purpose. Fortunately, many people do, and they get to share it with us like I'm doing here. My passion is to inspire others to find their purpose and pursue it with perseverance and determination. I get great satisfaction from helping others, whether people or businesses, to achieve objectives beyond what they thought was possible. There will be obstacles in life, guaranteed. Let those challenges propel you into greatness and strength. Someone or something may be trying to bring you down. That might even be yourself! Many psychiatrists call this our own inner darkness. It is real and it is there. You need to search deep inside to find the light within you. There is a certain force within all of us that is waiting to be explored into greatness. It will seem that the voice of inner darkness is the easier path forward. It usually is. However, I do hope that you make the choice that is right for you and for your loved ones. The choice that brings you happiness and warmth. That is usually the harder path, or that road less traveled.

I sincerely hope you know that there is help along the way and many people who care. As I capture my life's experiences here, hopefully you've realized that nothing is accomplished in solitude. There was help from people who cared, people who were ready to make an impact in someone else's life. At times, these angels or support systems may not be readily in front of you. It may mean that we have to look for them. We have to reach out and find whatever help is needed at the time. You will find answers through people, through resources, and many times, through your own self-reflection. I encourage you to reach out and let others propel you to the greater heights that you deserve. I would greatly enjoy comparing stories and helping you with your journey to excellence. You have my contact information in the About the Author section of this book.

As I wrap up this last chapter, in my own self-reflection, I know that I have grown tremendously through my many life experiences, the ups and downs and tribulations of life. I ask that you take the next step in identifying what excites you the most and pursue that passion with perseverance. As you do this, expect bumps, bruises, setbacks, mistakes, and many lessons learned. Know that we all have them. This, I believe, is what makes the mystery of life beautiful and intriguing all at once. You really never know what's coming next. However, if you stay true to your passions, you will overcome adversity and prevail. These experiences will make you stronger, so embrace them. They are excellent opportunities that will enable you to conquer your fears and enable you to grow and move forward. In turn, I hope that you also pay it forward, and help one other person, group, or organization. You're the hero of your own story! I encourage you to share your story.

I end with one simple question for you: Are you ready to ignite your passion?

Let's do this!

# Appendix
# MOM'S RECIPES!

# HOW TO MAKE MEXICAN RICE

## INGREDIENTS:

2 tablespoons of vegetable oil
1 cup of Mexican rice
¼ chopped white onion
4 finely chopped garlic cloves
1 teaspoon of ground cumin
2 tablespoons of tomato bouillon with chicken flavor
4 cups of water
½ of a 15 oz can of mixed vegetables

## INSTRUCTIONS:

Grab an 11 × 2 inch frying pan.
With the frying pan over medium heat, fry the white rice with the vegetable oil.
Keep frying until the rice is slightly brown in color, making sure not to burn it. There should be some spots of white and light brown on the rice grains.
Add the chopped garlic cloves, the chopped onion, the ground cumin, and the tomato bouillon to the lightly brown-colored rice.
Add four cups of water to the rice and spices.
Add the mixed vegetables and cover the frying pan under medium heat to bring everything to a slow boil.
After the water has boiled, turn down the heat to low and let it simmer for 15 minutes.
Once the water has fully evaporated, the Mexican rice is ready to eat!
Enjoy!

# HOW TO MAKE FLOUR TORTILLAS

# HOW TO MAKE FLOUR TORTILLAS

## INGREDIENTS:

1 ½ cups water (you will boil 3, but only need to use about 1 ½ cups)
1 pound white flour
4 tablespoons all-vegetable shortening
¼ teaspoon baking power
⅛ teaspoon salt

## INSTRUCTIONS:

Boil 3 cups of water.
Grab a large bowl, minimum size: 12 inches in diameter, 5 inches in height.
Place 1 pound of white flour in the bowl.
Add 4 tablespoons of all-vegetable shortening.
Add ¼ teaspoon baking powder.
Add ⅛ teaspoon salt.
Add 1 ½ cups hot water.

Knead it really, really well by hand.
Make dough patties 2.5 inches in diameter × 0.5 inches in height.
Let the patties sit for 30 minutes.

Roll them into circular tortilla shapes with a rolling pin. If they turn out more like the Texas state or any other state map, that's okay. Don't stress—I guarantee you the taste is the same. Place them on a hot griddle or nonstick pan until both sides are well done which will take about 30 to 45 seconds on each side. You know they are done when they are slightly golden brown or beige in color with brown spots throughout.

Enjoy!

# HOW TO MAKE DELICIOUS TAMALES

## INGREDIENTS:

2 pounds of dried corn husks for tamales
Water—enough to cover the corn husks fully in whatever container you choose

## SPICE MIX:

1 garlic head—the entire head of garlic cloves will be used
1 tablespoon cumin seeds
1 tablespoon pepper balls
Water—enough to cover the spices is sufficient

## CHICKEN:

10 pounds of chicken parts
Water—enough to fully cover the chicken parts
(save the chicken broth)

## RED CHILI:

9 ounces Ancho Chili dried red peppers
2 ¼ cups of water

## TAMALE DOUGH:

10 pounds corn tortilla dough—this is best when it's in plain dough form, as if you're going to make corn tortillas
1 ½ pounds pork lard
1 tablespoon salt
¼ cup spice mix from above

## RED CHILI CHICKEN:

Boiled chicken from above
Red chili mix from above
6 ounces chicken broth from above
2 tablespoons salt

## RED CHILI FLAVORED BEANS:

2 pounds of pinto beans
2 quarts of water
¼ cup salt for pot of beans
½ cup red chili mix from above

1. Place the corn husks in hot water with a heavy bowl or any weight on top for softening the husks. An hour of soaking in hot water is best to ensure they are soft and pliable.

2. Prepare the spice mix:
    In a small cup blender, or a full-size blender (but just know that if a full-size blender, you will have a lot of empty space), place the several peeled cloves of garlic from one garlic head in the blender. Make sure the garlic cloves are perfectly peeled.
    Add 1 tablespoon of cumin seeds.
    Add 1 tablespoon of black pepper balls.
    Cover these spices with water—enough water to cover them is sufficient.
    Blend until it becomes a well-blended, viscous mix and place it aside in a separate dish once blended.

3. Prepare the chicken:
   Boil 10 pounds of chicken parts in a large pot.
   Save 1 liter of the boiled chicken broth for later use.
   After boiling, shred the entire chicken into very small pieces.

4. Prepare the red chili mix:
   Remove all seeds from the red chili pods.
   Boil 9 ounces of the red chili pods.
   Blend ¾ cup of water with 2 cups of red chili until smooth, add another ¾ cup water and another 2 cups of red chili, add last ¾ cup of water and 2 cups of red chili.
   Set aside the red chili mix in a separate bowl. Note—this mix may stain your bowl, so a glass bowl or a similar colored bowl is best.

5. Prepare the tamale dough:
   Put 10 pounds of corn tortilla dough in a very large bowl.
   Add 1 ½ pounds pork lard.
   Add 1 tablespoon salt.
   Add ½ cup red chili mix from above.
   Add ¼ cup spice mix from above.
   Knead the dough well with your hands until everything is well mixed and the dough is soft with a red tint to it. Be sure to remove all finger jewelry, and you may wear disposable plastic gloves for kneading the dough, although it's easiest to do without gloves.

6. Prepare the red chili chicken:
    Boil the 10 pounds shredded chicken with 6 ounces of chicken broth.
    Add 2 ½ cups of red chili mix.
    Add another 6 ounces of chicken broth.
    Add 2 tablespoons of salt.
    Boil and mix until everything is well mixed.
    Remove from heat and set aside.

7. Prepare the red chili pinto beans:
    In a large pot, add 2 quarts of water.
    Add 2 pounds of pinto beans.
    Add ¼ cup salt.
    Boil the beans and add water as needed. Let it boil for about 1 ½ to 2 hours until the pinto beans are brown and soft.
    Smash the beans and add ½ cup of red chili mix, combine well, then set aside.

8. Now you're ready to spread the masa (tamale dough) onto the damp and soft corn husks. You should look for the soft shiny side once you remove the corn husks from the water and spread the dough onto this shiny side using a spoon or a spatula. This is the process where you call any family members, friends, or extended family members that want to hangout, tell jokes, or stories and you just make it a fun and engaging experience. From the looks of the quantity of damp corn husks and tamale dough, you'll be here for a while.

9. After you spread the dough onto the corn husk, fill it with either the red chili chicken mix or the red chili bean mix and wrap it up like a tiny gift. Fill it like a taco, then fold both sides of the corn husk around the chicken or bean mix, then fold the top edge backward so that the wrapping stays in place.

10. After spreading and preparing all the tamales with either chicken or beans, you are ready to cook them. First place about 5 to 8 damp corn husks or any remaining pieces of damp corn husks onto the bottom of a very large pot. Then place the tamales over the damp corn husks and stack them nicely on top of each other. Depending on the size of the pot, about ⅓ to ½ of the tamales out of the 10 pounds of dough may fit in there. If it is about half of them, add 3 cups of water to the pot and set them to boil for about 45 to 60 minutes. Check them after 45 minutes and ensure they are well cooked. If the masa is still runny or not well cooked, leave them on for another 15 minutes. Continue to check for doneness until they are soft and well cooked.

Enjoy your delicious tamales!

# ACKNOWLEDGEMENTS

I'd like to thank the entire team at Palmetto Publishing who made this book possible. Everyone's attention to detail and critical review with a watchful eye and a caring heart made this a pleasant and memorable experience. They made the process so simple that I'm preparing for my next book! Thank you, Palmetto Team!

I also want to thank my caring and powerful mentors that continue to inspire me and challenge me every day. Adam Coffey, JT Foxx, and Marcia Avedon, thank you for taking the time to guide me throughout life, and to perfect the final touches to my story. Your review and contributions will forever be appreciated. I hope to inspire others through this memoir as you all have inspired me.

# ABOUT THE AUTHOR

Griselda is a Mexican-American Latina mother to three amazing children, and happy wife to her husband, Greg. They currently live on the Space Coast in Melbourne, Florida, enjoy watching Gregory and Gabriela play sports, and support Briana in her first job at AstraZeneca after college graduation in May 2024. Griselda was born and raised in the border town of Brownsville, Texas. She graduated from Stanford University with an industrial engineering degree, from Arizona State University with an MBA, and after twenty-nine years working in corporate America, she started her own consulting business focused on team productivity and high performance coaching called Lean Business Excellence. Her passion is to empower people and businesses to thrive and achieve their full potential.

In business, she is an operations executive leader with proven success generating multimillion dollar savings for companies' bottom line to facilitate rapid growth. She has solid experience across twenty-six countries leading cross-cultural teams as a transformational leader in the global deployment of continuous improvement and lean principles.

She is one of the original developers of operational excellence frameworks for Fortune 500 companies Honeywell, Ingersoll Rand, Trane Technologies, and L3Harris

Technologies. Her proficiency in driving a continuous improvement culture and improving business performance across the enterprise by leveraging her Lean Master and Six Sigma certifications is exemplary.

She achieved success in three joint venture start-ups, eight greenfield/brownfield lean site designs, and sixteen successful site/product transitions. Her specialty is to establish and lead a continuous improvement vision and strategy as she did for these companies that led to significant operating income savings. She describes herself as an authentic, servant leader who loves working with people and teams. Her top strength is engaging people in transformational change to achieve breakthrough performance with a common vision.

She can be reached at griselda@businesscoachingresults.com or connect via
LinkedIn: www.linkedin.com/in/griselda-abousleman
Facebook: www.facebook.com/griselda.abousleman
Instagram: @griselda.excellence
www.businesscoachingresults.com